WARNING! IF YOU ARE SEEN
HOLDING OR READING THIS
BOOK, YOUR ADVERSARIES WILL
WONDER WHAT YOU KNOW
AND MAY BECOME EVEN MORE
ADVERSARIAL AS A RESULT.

PRAISE FOR
Escaping the School Leader's Dunk Tank

"*Escaping the School Leader's Dunk Tank tackles challenges that school leaders will face at some point in their careers. This book provides a unique and thorough analysis of types of adversarial conditions, and the powerful stories that the authors collected from school leaders across the nation will provide leaders a chance to reflect, plan, and think about how they might prevail in their roles.*"

—TODD WHITAKER,
PROFESSOR AT INDIANA STATE UNIVERSITY,
INTERNATIONALLY RECOGNIZED EDUCATION EXPERT,
AND AUTHOR OF MORE THAN 40 BOOKS,
INCLUDING *WHAT GREAT PRINCIPALS DO DIFFERENTLY*

"*This book doesn't just address the elephant in the room; it rides it out of the room! A very REAL look at school politics and typical adversarial conditions that leaders face along with practical tools for thriving in any school leadership role.*"

—ANNETTE BREAUX,
INTERNATIONAL EDUCATIONAL EXPERT AND
AUTHOR OF *THE TEN-MINUTE INSERVICE*

"*I'm calling a home run right now! Bold, unconventional, and arguably the 'realest' school leadership book you will ever read. Rebecca Coda and Rick Jetter definitely don't pull any punches. With riveting case studies that highlight the good, the bad, and the ugly . . . I've never read a more honest assessment of politics in education and how to rise above the perils to pursue excellence for kids. Escaping the School Leaders' Dunk Tank is one of those rare books that you won't want to end.*"

—BRAD GUSTAFSON,
2016 NAESP DISTINGUISHED PRINCIPAL AWARD WINNER
AND AUTHOR OF *RENEGADE LEADERSHIP*

"Looking at the six years where I have been an administrator and the last five years as a principal, it does get lonely at the top. The feeling that someone is always criticizing your every move is palpable, and the isolation effect of the position breeds the feeling of a closed space. This book highlights many of the hard lessons I have learned about school leadership, especially in being a very young administrator. To put the leadership position into a focused context is a moment of relived experience in every word that is read, and any aspiring administrator would be best served to read this book over and over again. In fact, I would highly recommend this book to any school leader, seasoned or neophyte. Rick and Rebecca have come up with practical, yet meaningful, strategies to leverage this dream position to build better relationships, rise above all of the exigent factors that make the job nearly impossible, and have the feeling of success that came with first being named to the job return in spades!"

—ROB BUECHE,
PRINCIPAL,
FLINT COMMUNITY SCHOOLS

"We have all been dunked before! If you have ever even tried to be a leader in a school, then you know the feeling. This book will make you feel like you are not alone. It is a great, practical read for any educator in any system. A great collection of real life examples."

—JENNIFER FOX,
SCHOOL IMPROVEMENT AND
DATA/ASSESSMENT CONSULTANT

"Rules are meant to be broken. Jetter and Coda share stunning vignettes uncovering educational politics; the candor shocking. A must-read for aspiring educational leaders."

—CATHERINE BARRETT, M.ED.,
ARIZONA MASTER TEACHER COACH,
PHOENIX UNION HIGH SCHOOL DISTRICT

ESCAPING THE
SCHOOL LEADER'S

DUNK
TANK

HOW TO PREVAIL WHEN OTHERS
WANT TO SEE YOU DROWN

Rebecca Coda & Rick Jetter

Escaping the School Leader's Dunk Tank
© 2016 by Rebecca Coda and Rick Jetter

This book is available at special discounts when purchased in quantity for use as premiums, promotions, fundraisers, or for educational use. For inquiries and details, contact the publisher at shelley@daveburgessconsulting.com.

Published by Dave Burgess Consulting, Inc.
San Diego, CA
http://daveburgessconsulting.com

Cover Design by Genesis Kohler
Editing and Interior Design by My Writers' Connection

The chapter icons were designed by Vectors Market (A Business Letter), Daniel Bruce (Ch. 3), Vignesh Oviyan (Ch. 9), Madebyoliver (Ch. 13), with all others (except the target and DBC logo) by Freepik from Flaticon.com.

Library of Congress Control Number: 2016961170
Paperback ISBN: 978-0-9969896-6-4
Ebook ISBN: 978-0-9969896-7-1

First Printing: December 2016

To all of our friends and colleagues who have a hell of a time trying to lead others while their adversaries plot, pillage, and plunder.

WHAT'S INSIDE?

DISCLAIMER:

THE STORIES AND TESTIMONIES USED WITHIN THIS BOOK HAVE BEEN PROTECTED BY PSEUDONYMS IN ORDER TO SAFEGUARD THE RIGHTS AND ANONYMITY OF THOSE WHO PARTICIPATED IN SHARING THEIR STORIES WITH US. ANY SIMILARITIES TO REAL-LIFE NAMES, LOCATIONS, AND TITLES ARE MERELY COINCIDENCE.

PUSHING AN ELEPHANT FROM THE REAR

IT REQUIRED A LITTLE covert action, but the thrill of setting free the massive elephants at the carnival was worth the risk. We walked around back and saw their enclosure. To our surprise there was no lock on the cage, so we lifted the lever and called them all out. Thankfully, no one saw us when we released the elephants from their cages. That's when things really got interesting. We each grabbed onto an elephant, climbed up their enormous bodies, and sat upon their backs. They tried to buck us off, like angry bulls, and even smacked us across the faces with their heavy trunks. But when we fed them peanuts, they calmed down and let us ride them around inside the carnival tent. What an awesome experience!

The field of education is a little like our trip to the carnival, and it is filled with political elephants that buck and swat at us. The educators who dare to write books about those elephants typically end up with a manuscript casualty that—after enduring repeated rejections from publishers—ultimately dies, alone and unread on a dusty bookshelf. The reason? Publishers can be a lot like carnies with strict rules and procedures. Push the elephants out in the open and make them stroll around the carnival grounds so everyone can see them up close and personal? That just will not do! So after taking months and months to review a manuscript, they demand it be revised until it fits into their stuffy, academic molds (cages). You know those books—they are the ones that keep the carnival running at status quo.

Don't get us wrong. We read lots of books from lots of publishers. Some of these books help educators, but some stink. Some of them are memorable; others aren't. We wrote this book because we wished someone along the way would have provided a "dunk tank" leadership survival guide for us. We wished someone, *anyone*, would have pointed to the elephant in the room and talked about adversarial politics in education, the adversarial conditions that we were going to face, and how we needed to learn about *and from* these experiences in order to not drown, but swim freely.

Then we met Dave and Shelley Burgess. We love the books Dave Burgess Consulting, Inc. publishes. They are the kind of books that push elephants' rears and ruffle feathers by saying what needs to be said. They provide educators with practical wisdom and actionable advice, and they shove nothing in the closet. Elephants don't fit into closets, by the way, but you know that. We thought that Dave and Shelley Burgess would want to take a look at *Escaping the School Leader's Dunk Tank*. And they did, obviously. A huge thank you goes out to Dave and Shelley for being bold enough to join alongside us and push the elephants out into the open.

We are both dunk tank survivors. At one point in our careers as school leaders, we sank to the bottom of the school leaders' dunk tank. We made our escape, and now we are free. We are happy. We are stable. We are still friendly, and even stronger and smarter. We are indebted to our families, friends, and dunk tank spouses, Jennifer and Mike, for swimming with us with their life preservers and water wings.

Every day, more educators fall victim to the dunk tank. It's a place where they feel ridiculed and humiliated by leaders whose egos are bigger than elephants' rears. These *leaders* are power hungry or are just waiting for their fifty-fifth birthday so that they can collect their pensions. The worst of them would never consider for even two seconds how poorly they treat people along the way. Others are like the carnies maintaining the status quo. They are not bad people, but are simply ignorant of how their actions limit those who work with them. Our goal with this book is to help school leaders everywhere escape the dunk tank and join forces to revolutionize education. We want to team up with educators to expose the elephants that are jam-packed in schools, districts, and universities everywhere. Elephants come in all shapes and sizes, and have different kinds of tusks and goals. Some elephants are backstabbing coworkers, troubled or jealous supervisors, or even school board members who are out to get you. Lethal elephants often pound the pavement and turn schools or districts upside down—even at the cost of students—yet no one pushes on them. But we do. We also hope you will hand a copy of this book to someone who is making your professional life miserable. That way, they can see what you are learning from this book. It is a polite way to call out your adversaries' poor behaviors and shine a spotlight on the elephants in the room.

We are honored that you have picked up this book. We hope that it will embolden you to find a way to release the elephants from their political cages and push them out into the open for everyone to see. We are your fellow elephant-riding colleagues.

Don't get us wrong—we like animals. We love elephants. They are awesome. We just hate the metaphorical ones that sit quietly in the corner of education that no one dares to move— or even acknowledge.

WELCOME TO DUNK TANK UNIVERSITY

WE TYPED THE KEYWORDS "failed leadership," "poor leadership," "political leadership," and "leadership dunk tank" into the Amazon search bar to see what we would get. We even threw in the words "failed school leaders." We purposely kept the product scroll bar set at "All Departments," not just "Books." Some search results spit out products for tank tops for women, an "outstanding leadership" round charm necklace, and, of course, a Soak 'N' Wet stand-up dunk tank, as well as books about the armed forces and military-tank operation.

Then, there was a series of "we'll show you how to be a great leader" books, along with dozens of books and chapters written about dealing with difficult people, difficult teachers, difficult spouses, and difficult you-name-it. We are not poking fun at these titles. Rather, we contend that no one has ever written an in-your-face book about *adversarial* school leadership experiences due to human factors and conditions that you either currently face or will face someday as a school leader.

We wrote this book for all school leaders, district leaders, charter school leaders, university leaders leading leaders, teacher leaders, teachers aspiring to be leaders, etc. within *all kinds* of educational leadership fields: curriculum, special education, leadership, human resources, technology, athletics, etc. No one is immune to chaotic politics, adversarial conditions, or leadership assassinations in schools across America. It sounds totally *insane*, doesn't it? The words "adversarial conditions" and "education" don't belong in the same sentence.

Something interesting out there is also happening: teachers, parents, and even college graduates have taken an interest in why we wrote this book and what it teaches them about schools and school systems. Our hope (and theirs) is to galvanize our interconnectedness and common interest in making schools better places for children, instead of maintaining the status quo of schools as adult battlegrounds where children are a second thought. But please remember: We are not school *bashers*. We are writing this book to help as many people as we can across all walks of life, in schools everywhere.

You will not find a secret recipe or golden set of rules for success within these pages. Success as a school leader cannot be distilled into a simple *equation*. What you will find is actionable advice, powerful stories, and lessons to be learned. We share *real* stories from *real* school leaders with *real* experiences that will help you. Yes, *you*! This book contains raw, unfiltered, no-sugar-coating *real* events that happened to *real* educators. Our reason for sharing these stories is to ensure that you are successful in the field of education. We want to equip you as emerging and existing school leaders so you are prepared for every possible contingency as you climb the leadership ladder. From principal to superintendent, from site-based to the district office, or from the classroom to a teacher-leader role, each step up the ladder demands that you acquire new skillsets and a new way of thinking. We want you to be prepared for the day that revenge or jealousy taps you on the shoulder. Otherwise, what will you do when your livelihood is threatened and you have no real way out? Or when your adversaries celebrate your downfall? Or when you simply *crack*?

The phenomenon of *politics in education* and adversarial conditions are growing more rampant as education is faced with unrealistic obstacles. The lack of state and federal funding, changing standards that require new skillsets, the depletion of training and resources, and the additional pressures to advance in STEM (without even preparing our teachers) all impact the day-to-day life and stress levels of education leaders. The difficulties inherent in education today poke, provoke, and add a prolific amount of stress to educators. These conditions can bring out the worst in someone who may otherwise have been a *good* leader. So much is going on in education nowadays, and fiery emotions and villain-like tactics fly at school leaders from every direction!

The pressures are real, the expectations are high, and the funding is low. As in any organization, there are some people who will use the system for what they want: money, employment, power, or control. Many people (from parents to those in politics and the media) believe they can do what we were trained to do *better*. The result: Sometimes, school leaders become lepers. Sometimes they fail. Sometimes they do not know how to respond. Sometimes the stress feels overwhelming. *In a school?* Yes. In a school.

We have spoken to countless school leaders who felt they were strong enough to overcome any obstacle that stood in their way. None of them . . . not *one* of them . . . forecasted failure for themselves at any point within their career in education. Let us reiterate: We as humans do not forecast failure or treachery for ourselves. Why? Because we aren't trained to think that way. We all want to believe that educational systems are safe places for the teaching and learning of children. We want to believe this when we get out of bed each morning until we have eyes wide shut and sometimes feel like we have entered the *Twilight Zone*.

It is easy to slip on our "leader clothes" and fail to remember that we are all fallible beings who reside within our "human clothes" first. We are all prone to screwing up and making terrible mistakes. We are all at risk of gripping the bottle of bourbon or pint of ice cream a little tighter each night. We want to help you—*before* you get to that point, *before* you *crack*.

We aren't going to tell you what great leaders do right while ignoring what great leaders do to mess up or lose their careers or reputations. We aren't going to sidestep the realities of what it can be like to lead and put up with some of the garbage that truly does exist within the American educational system.

We *are* going to share real stories from people who have been shoved into the dunk tank and escaped to not only survive, but learn to *thrive*. When you get to the end of this book, you will feel invigorated and liberated because you will have learned all the strokes that help you escape the dunk tank and beat them at their own game.

Suit up. Grab your water wings and goggles, and let's dive in!

I didn't really lose a friend . . .
I just realized that I miscalculated.
—**MARK TWAIN**

A BUSINESS LETTER

Dear Adversaries:

We're sure you are probably stewing a bit that this book has been published. On the flipside, you are probably happy that we're still thinking about you. Well, we have to admit that we're still thinking about you, yes, but *differently* now. We hope that you can find peace in your lives, and we no longer carry around the burden of not being able to forgive you for what you did to us or our colleagues, even though you might still be trying to put the last nail in our professional coffins. See, that's the *difference*. We are thinking about *you* so we can help *others* who are forced to deal with their own adversaries.

You may even, deep down inside, still like us. Perhaps you appreciate our strong moral character and talent. And we recognize that your bad behavior may have been rooted in the desire for self-preservation. You didn't intentionally attempt to destroy us or our colleagues; that's just the way things worked out.

Had we been prepared with the knowledge and strategies presented in this book, if we had known all about challenging leadership realities, then, yes, we would have changed our tactics and interactions. We too should have responded differently along the way. We know now that school leadership should, like a chess game, be played strategically, thoughtfully, and reflectively. At the time, we did not have the tools to navigate what we call *extreme adversarial conditions*.

Countless other educated professionals became your adversaries; they are now our allies and have joined us in fighting the good fight for students across the nation. There is strength and unity in bountiful numbers. And be warned: We are working to strengthen leaders of all kinds so we are better prepared for leadership life while coping with you—because people like you will always exist. We've accepted that reality, and now we're aware of and equipped to diffuse the career land mines you set up for us. So thanks for the training. Whether or not it was your intention, we're better for it.

Best wishes,

R. Coda   Rick Jetter
Rebecca Coda   Rick Jetter

cc: School leaders everywhere

You must never be fearful about what you are doing when it is right.
—ROSA PARKS

CHAPTER 1

THE GREATEST PROFESSION ON EARTH

M*y mantra about kids was stapled to my wall. It was in large print, bright-red die-cut letters glued onto a five-foot-long piece of yellow butcher paper outlined with the cutest polka-dot border ever sold. My mantra was simple enough for every person who entered my room to understand:* **Do what's right, give it your best, because life is the most meaningful test.** *I expected this of my students, my parents, my nurses, my administrators, anyone who entered my room . . . we were a community of difference-makers, of dreamers, and our kids deserved that every adult in their life embraced and believed in this mantra.*

I wanted to ensure success for each and every student I had the privilege of teaching. I had the best job in the world working with special-education students who were medically fragile and cognitively disadvantaged. They were blessings entrusted to me. Joey was on a feeding tube and blind. Casey was epileptic and had Rett's syndrome. Donavan was a little person with a rare heart condition. All my kids were on special diets, confined to wheelchairs, had alternative standards, and needed specialized teaching that most people would take for granted. Often times, my room smelled of diaper changes, dietary foods, and antiseptic cleaners, but that isn't what I remember most.

What I remember most are the smallest breakthroughs. I remember what it felt like to communicate through eye gazes, smiles, therapeutic milestones, self-feeding, and pride. My kids were capable, and I believed in them. My heart was protective of each and every one of them. Their parents entrusted me to mold, guide, and teach them. I was honored. And that's why I gave 110 percent every day with my very heart and soul. After all, I had chosen the greatest profession on earth. The most fulfilling profession. A profession of impact. A profession that mattered. That's why I'm an educator, and that's my elevator speech. I care about kids. I'm a kid advocate, and I will do nothing less than to help every child (and adult) succeed. Educators have been bred to do what's right and give it their best, knowing that life is the most meaningful test. That's the formula for success in my classroom anyway.

—SYLVIA ANDERSON,
ASSISTANT SUPERINTENDENT, WEST VIRGINIA

If you are in education, you understand what an honor it is to teach. We are in the business of changing the future, impacting lives, and empowering people. What we do matters. It directly impacts those around us. Sylvia lives by the idealistic principles of gratitude and fulfillment. Her heart was happy knowing that she lived her own mantra.

You probably started your first year of teaching with a passion for embracing obstacles, working through challenges, and being solution-oriented (sometimes repeating that cycle every thirty seconds). Perhaps you have had some really gratifying experiences at some point in your teaching career. But that may not be where you are now. If you have moved on to instructional coaching, administration, district leadership, university level teaching, or act as an educational consultant supporting the teaching industry, you may be far removed from the classroom and the heart-warming, satisfying learning experiences that occur there. If you have been out of the classroom for some time now, you may not feel like you are the best educator-version of yourself. Can you honestly say that you are more on fire than you ever have been in your career? Or have you lost a little bit of your "best self" along the way as you've coped with the stress of leading others? Whether you are on top of your game, or struggling to decide if you even want to remain in education, we want to remind you that you are part of the best profession on earth. How you respond to the struggles, challenges, darts, and arrows hurtling at you affects you—and everyone around you.

LEADERSHIP ISN'T A JOB

When you do what is right and give it your best, leadership is the most meaningful test. It's *who you are.* It flows through your veins. Leadership is all-encompassing. You don't need a name plate on your office door to remind you who you are. You don't need stationary with bold lettering denoting your title or position. Those material symbols might create an artificial feeling of *important-ness*, but to exemplify true leadership—to really make a difference—you have to do what's right and give it your best, just as Sylvia expected of her students.

We've been through the *manufactured* glory of being a leader in our past careers. Newspapers. Media. Shaking hands and kissing babies. Facilitating leadership meetings. Evaluating performance. Coordinating district events. Spotlights. Speeches. Leading individuals. Leading large crowds. Making people laugh. Making them feel good about what they do even when they feel like they hate what they do.

Yet we've made tons of mistakes . . . career-crippling mistakes. We've been knocked down by adversaries, and we've let our leadership positions go to our heads at times. The good news is that we can recognize where we've been, what we could have done differently, and then transform those learning experiences into wisdom that we can share.

Unfortunately, behind the district curtain lies a world that our profession should be ashamed of, and these are the stories that grieve us. These are the unspoken stories about adversarial situations that can make or break an entire school, district, county, or state.

YOU ARE ALREADY SITTING ON THE PLATFORM OF ADVERSITY

All of you as leaders are sitting on a metaphorical platform that will fall right out from under you with one strike of the target. Your adversaries want to see you or your colleagues drown, and there might not be anything you can do to change the emotional forces and behaviors driving their actions. But you can prepare yourself to escape (rather than sink) by deciding how you will respond, how you should act, and how you should lead.

The unfortunate reality is that the poor attitudes of others are difficult to remediate. We realize that this sounds pessimistic and absolute, but toxic people are everywhere. Maybe you already know who they are. Or maybe they have not arrived at your doorstep—yet. They might be visible or invisible. Flagrant or feeble. Overt or covert. Two-faced or in-your-face. But they are out there.

Life is not perfect, and no one is lucky enough to be liked by everyone. Dunk Tank graduates fully understand that doing what is right will instill emotions of honor in some, while initiating feelings of hatred in others.

Now that you have realized that this book is about *your* adversaries within education, it may conjure up some strong feelings of resentment, anger, and retaliation. That's natural; but we encourage you not to label your adversaries as *enemies*. Oh sure, you can call them any venomous name you want—hypocrites, back-stabbers, ignorant fools. But by holding on to that negativity, you are only hurting your own spirit. Any lack of forgiveness on your part will be *your* burden to carry. Those who confronted you or tried to make your life miserable will go about their lives with virtually no impact.

The first prerequisite to entering Dunk Tank University is that you must believe that all people are good—or at least that everyone has some goodwill still left within their bones. The second prerequisite is to understand that, for some adversaries, no art or science of persuasion will ever turn them into allies. But we sure are going to give it our best shot. Regardless of your adversary's character (or lack thereof), you will be able to sleep well at night knowing that you maintained excellence, remained fearless of doing what's right, and did it all for the belief that kids deserve better.

You may have failed as a leader once, twice, or maybe even three times in your life. Right now, you might be looking back on all of the things *you* did wrong. Maybe you have moved from job to job in search of greener grass somewhere else as you secured a new school leadership position. You may have even been fired or forced to resign. Yes, this is an elephant, an unspeakable topic in education: Good people with hearts and performance like Sylvia can end up in the dunk tank without realizing how they got there. (This is why it's so important to believe that *all* people—even your adversaries—have good within them. You can help them find their way back to the light.)

You may feel like you are on top of the world right now. You might very well be a *terrific* leader, practicing the art and science of powerful and positive leadership skills, building trust, and gaining support. You might feel like everything is going just right.

Or you may be *that* leader who has the ego, mistrust, desire to abuse power, or the ignorance of all that is happening (for the worse) within your organization. (Or you may be doing terrible things and be completely oblivious to what is happening all around you.) Remember, it is not too late to change yourself, re-image, or re-create your organization.

Whatever your situation, this book is for you. Why? It is a *manual for preparedness.* And preparedness requires healthy anticipation and a bit of proactive paranoia.

IT'S HEALTHY TO BE (A LITTLE) PARANOID

There is no terror in a BANG . . .
only the anticipation of it.
—ALFRED HITCHCOCK

Allow us to present a concept to you that we call "proactive paranoia" or "healthy anticipation." First, let's go back to Sylvia, whose inspiring words opened this chapter. It is hard to believe that someone like Sylvia, who is the epitome of excellence in education, would ever face an adversary. Sylvia out-performed other special education teachers. She believed in her kids and went home every single night feeling fulfilled. Eventually, she made her way up the leadership hierarchy and is now an assistant superintendent. Take a look at a few more comments from Sylvia:

> *Sometimes I just think I'm crazy or wonder if it's just my imagination getting the best of me . . . but I feel like . . . like my superintendent is trying to get rid of me. I've been in this district for fourteen years, adore the students and staff here, and have become part of the community. I've made a lot of friends here. Even though I have tenure, I heard through the grapevine that my superintendent wants to abolish my position. That's the only way he can get rid of me, technically. One of his best friends is looking for a job as a director of special education, and I think they are going to get rid of me in order to bring him in. I try to think about what I did to upset the superintendent, but I just don't know. I just think he doesn't like me and wants to get his friend a job. It sounds so silly, but I feel*

like the writing is on the wall. My superintendent just loaded me up with seven additional projects on top of my other duties because I think he's setting me up for failure. I lose sleep every night. I work about fifteen or sixteen hours a day. I'm the first one in and the last one out, but it doesn't matter. My grave is being dug . . . and I don't know what to do. I thought I was in the kid business, not a cutthroat corporate world.

Sylvia's imagination is not running wild. She feels it in her gut that something is wrong. Body language, tone of voice, and comments made in jest have pinged on her *proactive paranoia radar.*

It may seem that there is nothing Sylvia can do. She believes her hands are tied by politics and power, and that's a common response. A typical leader may brush the feelings off and assume positive intent. After all, we have district values to uphold. Educators have a higher moral compass and ethical code, right? It may seem far-fetched that the superintendent was really trying to sabotage her career. It's easier to assume that because Sylvia is already overworked, stressed, and not sleeping well, her imagination has gotten the best of her. But that isn't a safe assumption.

Is she paranoid? Probably not.

Is there anything that she can do? Absolutely! (We will cover specific strategies and ideological practices in Chapters 7-10.)

It is the reality of dunk tank life that adversaries work to create environments and situations that are more about self-preservation and incompetency than anything else. Sylvia doesn't realize the traps that have been set; all she knows is that she has given her blood, sweat, and tears for the past fourteen years and now her superintendent wants her ousted. That well-founded fear has impacted her sense of self-worth as well as her efficacy. At the moment, she feels as if she is drowning at the bottom of the tank. She is suffocated to the point of anxiety, self-doubt, regret, sorrow, and many sleepless nights. She knows she isn't living by her own mantra because she has no more to give, and she knows that she is no longer at her best. Sylvia is fearful of the inevitable and sure that she's a goner. Sylvia doubts that she should even stay in her position. She *feels* paranoid and is in dire need of a game plan. She needs strategies and support systems to empower her next steps and free her from the illusion that she did anything wrong.

"Proactive paranoia" is not linked to a mental health condition or deficiency. Rather, we contend that there is a positive side of paranoia. Proactive paranoia is the *anticipation* of problems, negative reactions or responses of others, or a constructive, thorough process by which one plans and implements safeguards for ensuring security, peacefulness, or contextual integrity. It allows you to employ CYA (cover-your-ass) measures even before it needs to be covered.

This type of paranoia is *healthy*. It's not about covering up mistakes, but rather, it's about getting ready for battle (in case *battling* is inevitable). Think beyond suits of armor or Kevlar vests. You may need to get ready for *something* to go wrong within your organization, because your leadership might turn sour even if you have great intentions and didn't really do anything wrong in the first place. The guard changes often in education. New school board members are elected into office. Administrators come and go. Contracts are renegotiated. We might have different intentions about helping kids than our parent leaders have. Our own colleagues might be working against us when a promotion is up for grabs.

Proactive paranoia is situational and contextual. It is necessary for establishing a mindset of preparedness. It is not turned on and off during a situation or event—rather, it is *always* on. And it will allow you to navigate experiences and continually scan for trouble, pitfalls, or potential problems.

In fact, it is proactive paranoia that allowed Anna Li, a director of special education in New York, to prepare for a meeting that could have ended her career. Here are her candid feelings and what she did to suit up for that meeting:

> *They are coming for me . . . I know it. A parent who didn't like the outcome of a committee on special education meeting—and her friends [sigh]—will be at the board meeting tonight, I'm sure of it. I prepped the superintendent so she was aware of the situation, and I'm going to put together some executive session documents just in case they come tonight to lynch me. That way, I can show the board why the decision to not place a student in a 6:1:1 class is what's best for this child. The entire committee agreed. The data and child's history does not support a 6:1:1 placement. I'm going to bring all of the paperwork and data with me in my bag tonight just in case. I also saved the voicemail of the parent screaming at me at the top of her lungs. I can't let this parent bully us into what is not in the best interest of her child. The superintendent just wants to make this problem go away. I'm not sure where she is coming from, but at least I will be prepared tonight.*

While this example is not intended to vilify the superintendent, it is a good example of a real situation that happens in education, and it offers a proactive approach. Anna made sure she was prepared for anything that might happen at the board meeting or during the public comment section. While this situation is meant to only deal with doing what is best for the child, there is a potential dunk tank outcome, especially if the board and/or superintendent wanted this problem to "go away."

Clashing ideas about what is best for students or the system itself may become the sword that we are either going to die on or use to defend ourselves. The great controversy over doing what's right and political bargaining is nothing new for school leaders. It happens everywhere and more often than anyone will admit (yet another elephant in education). We are sometimes faced with difficult barriers where we are expected to balance politics with reality—while trying our hardest to do what's best for children.

As you read through this book, you will find more real stories of school leaders and the stress and challenges they have faced. Some of these stories may seem too absurd to be true, but truth is often stranger than fiction. From these leaders' experiences, you will glean realistic wisdom so that you can determine when it is healthy to leave an organization, how to stop trying to change others' behavior, and how to maintain your health and sanity.

We feel that educators are the most overworked and underpaid profession on the planet. Educators work more overtime than any other career with no compensation to support the additional time invested. The long hours and variety of continually changing demands create enough stress to sink someone. Add to that an adversary who constantly throws softballs at the dunk tank target just to see you drown, and it can be overwhelming.

Before we move any further, we would like you to embrace the following ten crucial tenets which we believe matter when working through adversarial realities in schools everywhere. Incorporating these ten crucial tenets into your current belief system will allow you to leverage your leadership. Read these ten crucial points out loud (yes, literally *out loud*) before moving forward with the rest of this book. You will have to commit to them in order to become a Dunk Tank Graduate, so you may as well memorize them now.

TEN CRUCIAL TENETS

1. I am a good leader. Good leaders are always in training no matter how long they've been leading.

2. I know that people, in general, have good intentions, are good natured, and really want to help others succeed.

3. I really do like what I do. If I ever stop enjoying my work, I will remember that moving on is always an option, never a settlement.

4. I am not oblivious to the reality that there are nasty people out there. I also understand that these people may try to bring me down for reasons that are only important to *them.*

5. I accept that my adversaries have their own intentions. Sometimes it will be impossible to change how they feel or what they want to do to "win" their battle.

6. If I don't activate powerful, mindful leadership safeguards (or elements of wisdom), I am unprotected and weak.

7. I cannot take anything personally—even if my adversaries' nuclear bombs and warfare *become* personal.

8. I am only as prepared as my *anticipations*.

9. If I forecast unbearable chaos, I must listen to my gut and, if necessary, abort or retreat my position or circumstances. If I feel like my leadership position is making me unhealthy, I need to seek healthy shores. This is also not to be considered "quitting," but rather "refitting" myself to where I need to be and what I need to do without having chaotic distractions in my life. I only get one life to live. I will not let others destroy my happiness.

10. I have a good heart; I don't mean to harm anyone, ever; and I don't desire to tread on anyone for any self-fulfilling reason. If I inadvertently hurt someone, I will apologize and try to make it right.

We want you to not simply tread water but rather to swim in the waters of positive leadership. Your adversaries may be hoping you drown after they smash the dunk tank target. They have a pocket of dollar bills and will purchase as many throws as necessary to watch you sink. You won't see the first hit coming unless you embrace proactive paranoia and anticipate their moves. You can master the art of prevailing in your leadership career. And as you learn to swim, you can help others too.

*A man who wants to lead
the orchestra must turn his
back on the crowd.*

—MAX LUCADO

CHAPTER 2

THE POWER OF EMOTIONS

I loved coming to work every day, especially on Tuesdays because that's the day the chemistry club met after school. One particular student, Travis, was a junior who took the lead in this club. He had a student seminar the last period of the day and would always come in early to my classroom to set up the lab, organize the materials, and go over the learning we were hoping would take place. I coached him on asking his peers probing questions rather than simply giving them the answers. I taught him to listen to what others were saying and also allow *everyone to make their own mistakes (as long as it wasn't endangering anyone). Not only was I teaching Travis the foundations of chemistry, I was teaching him to be a leader. He was already a 4.2 genius-student; his next step was to learn to lead others. I will always remember the day when I watched Travis address the club emulating the same questioning techniques and positive tone, while demonstrating the kindness that I expect in my classroom. It was a surreal moment; I felt as if I were looking at a younger version of myself. I knew that day, I had made a difference. My hope wasn't that Travis would be just like me, but that he would learn skills that would stay with him forever, even longer than the elements he had memorized on the periodic table. Travis was becoming a true leader, and I had given him that gift. That's why I am in education.*

—RUSS PATTERSON,
HIGH SCHOOL PRINCIPAL, NEW MEXICO

When we spoke to Russ, he was emotional—in a *good* way. He felt as though every long day he had spent as a teacher grading papers until ten o'clock at night, every parent phone call, every struggle he had worked through in class, and every classroom evaluation had value because Russ knew he was leaving his mark. He *knew* he was making a difference in others' lives.

People always have a reason for their actions—positive or negative. Always. Emotions often lie at the heart of those actions. Our research indicates that emotions run particularly high in educational organizations. And that makes sense. Schools are filled with people who have chosen the education profession because they want to make an impact. They don't do it for the money, respect, or recognition but rather for the contributions they can make to children's lives. Our profession is fueled by the emotions that cause people to care enough to make a *daily sacrifice* to help, teach, encourage, and mentor the next generation. It's likely that even our adversaries started out with a difference-maker's mindset. But somewhere along the way, something happened; and, as a result, they joined the varsity dunk tank team.

In this chapter, we'll identify some of the reasons issues such as leadership accusations and confrontations arise. We'll also offer a few strategic tactics that you may be able to use to diffuse emotionally charged situations.

Be warned: Even though members of the varsity dunk tank team may have started out with a mindset to help and encourage others, many of them have ventured down ruthless paths that led them to abuse the system or make their profession about them rather than kids. You might not be able to win them back to the difference-makers' team or diffuse their artillery, but it may still be possible to influence the situation and minimize the casualties. We'll talk more about that in Chapter 8.

WHY ARE THEY ACTING THIS WAY?!

People change for two main reasons.
Either their minds have been opened or
their hearts have been broken.
—STEVEN AILCHISON

People do not wake up one morning and just decide to be deceitful or problematic. No adversary chose to be in education for the sole purpose of ruining someone else's life or career. Nor did they join the varsity dunk tank team for fun. More likely,

17

they became educators because they believed in the dream of changing kids' lives. Whether you feel like believing it right now, your adversaries have hearts and souls. They also have reasons for their actions.

The question, then, is what is the reason? *Why do your adversaries do what they do?*

As we spoke with school leaders across the nation, one recurring theme resounded time and again: Adversaries' deeply-rooted, negative attitudes are (often) the result of experiences that made them feel victimized in some way. Their hurtful or spiteful behavior is often a response to, or the result of, such experiences and may have very little—if anything—to do with you personally. Some person or circumstance (or multiple people and circumstance) hurt them, and as a result they sharpened their adversarial skills along the way. They, like everyone else in the world, are driven by their emotions. Only, they operate (continually and irrationally) in emotional defense mode to avoid being hurt again. If they perceive you as a threat to their career or happiness, their emotions will drive them to obsess about bringing you down.

Emotional defense mechanisms vary and can include tactics such as questioning your leadership, denouncing your authority, or fighting your efforts. These emotional responses are common in any of life's adversarial interactions, but we find it particularly interesting that they occur so frequently and blatantly within the context of the educational system. We all know that negative student behaviors have a driving causal factor behind them; so do adult behaviors. It's that simple. In adversaries, the emotions caused by that hurtful experience drive primitive responses to situations. In fact, this is an adversarial prerequisite, and it fosters the negative governing emotions that drive their specific actions. Emotional dissonance, ego, and entitlement become by-products of this vicious cycle.

Sometimes the attitude-altering experience occurred long before our adversaries ever became educators. We have known adversarial leaders who were abused as children, or unloved or unwanted by their family, or told at a young age they would never succeed. Some rose out of extreme poverty, others were spoiled rotten as children. The fact of the matter is, we are all products of our past, and we all have the power to transform our future. The difference between you and your adversary is that he or she has a schema that distorts their view on life. It's as if they are carrying a gym bag filled with dunk tank practice balls and are just waiting for someone like you to step into their line of sight.

Whatever the root cause, adversaries have developed a hunger to succeed at any cost or the desire to abuse other people within their organization the same way someone abused or took advantage of them in their past lives. Adversaries come from all different backgrounds, but one commonality we discovered in our research was the attitude or desire to treat others as harshly or unfairly as they themselves had been treated. You see, people who have been hurt often hurt other people. It is what they know and what they have seen negatively modeled by others along the way. That's why a recurring theme in our school leaders' narratives is that the abuse of power, ego, nepotism, and self-preservation tactics all stem from an overcompensation or response to past experiences. Each person interviewed discussed how their "abuser" had experienced a negative experience in their past and, as a result, mistreated others in a similar fashion.

Some of these adversaries, which include other school leaders, did not "lead" with positive motives. They did not respond in such a way as to show that they had heart. They appeared cunning, ruthless, and disconnected from what was really happening within the organization. We refer to these adversaries as the "walking wounded" troop. We are hopeful that they will heal, but the wounds of their past may also fester and grow within them.

IDENTIFY THE EMOTIONAL TRIGGER

As a school leader, your own perception and state of mind are important. You must evaluate what *is* within your control and accept that some things, such as "fixing" another person, are out of your control. If you can identify your adversaries' emotional driving forces and then react in a manner that is strategic and rational, then you can prevent your adversaries from harming you or your organization.

Emotions drive human behavior and are (often) a response to external factors in life. That means when you're dealing with an adversary, *their* external factors (past or present) become your burden. In other words, to make it through the day, week, or month, you must survive your adversary's emotional roller coaster. Staying on a positive course and maintaining your own sanity requires that you wake up ready to deal with your adversary's debilitations day after day. Dealing with the "walking wounded" may require tip-toeing, stroking, complying, and even submission.

It helps to remember that your adversary is a product of dysfunction who is operating in a world of delusion, instability, and unhealthy paranoia. It is unlikely that your adversary is aware of how their behaviors affect you or anyone else. In fact, self-reflection probably seems too difficult for the "walking wounded" to face. Instead, stepping on others or destroying people in their organization is an easier path to reaching their goal. Remember, though, that destruction may not have been their initial goal. More likely, their original intention was self-preservation. Their behavior may be more about responding to feelings of inadequacies. To the "walking wounded," you are perceived as a threat. When this happens, no matter the trigger, they lash out at you, causing you to feel defenseless, helpless, or, even worse, relentlessly angry.

In this section, we'll examine a few key emotions that may trigger negative feelings in your adversary. It is vital to figure out what makes your adversary "tick" because determining the root cause for your adversary's behavior will help you respond appropriately. In the best-case scenario, understanding their motives and emotions may allow you to cultivate positive relationships with them. If nothing else, you will be better equipped to deal with them as you move your organization forward.

Keep in mind that the following human emotions don't always breed adversaries who are after you as a leader or who hate your leadership. Every person is different, and every "walking wounded" adversary requires a special key to unlock their motives, navigate their behaviors, and stealthily steer them in a more positive direction. You can look at it as positive manipulation or simply as helping someone with an emotional disability, generated by their past experiences, that is preventing them from overcoming their emotions. Consider this additional story from our chemistry teacher, Russ, who is now a third-year principal:

> I've been a good leader. I've done my job. But now that the board of education changed over and includes those who hate my boss [the superintendent], I'm on the ropes too. Why? Because he hired me. That's why. I'm his hire; therefore, I'm going to be their fire. They want to cauterize anyone who is linked to him. They aren't going to stop,

either. It's already begun. His contract is going to expire next year. There is no way they'll renew it—and for no good reason. I have no idea why they want him out; and if they want him out, there is no way I'll ever receive tenure. I know I have to start looking for a job. I'm under a microscope, and they are just waiting for something to complain about. The other day, I had to run an emergency drill because of a potential barrier that was created at our main entrance due to some capital project work taking place on the roof. Some wood and tiles fell near the door. Stuff almost hit Mrs. Nelson, one of our parents. She got so upset and told the board on me. Like I didn't care or something. But now the board thinks that I don't have a safety plan for the capital project work. Like I'm a sap or something.

—RUSS PATTERSON,
HIGH SCHOOL PRINCIPAL, NEW MEXICO

Russ doesn't know why the new school board wants him out, nor does he know why his superintendent is in the same boat.[1] What he does know is that he is linked to the superintendent as one of his supporters and, therefore, he is too close to the superintendent for the board to want him to stick around. As a result, Russ feels as if he is being scrutinized. Life for Russ is miserable.

The following emotions are among those that drive adversarial behavior. When you notice any of these emotions directed toward you, your proactive paranoia should kick in. We've listed them in no particular order; however, some might seem more powerfully detrimental to leaders and their leadership pursuits than others.

---

1   For more information about adversarial school boards, see Spencer, M. (2013). *Exploiting Children: School Board Members Who Cross the Line*. New York: Rowman and Littlefield.

JEALOUSY

*Jealousy is no more than feeling alone
against smiling enemies.*
—ELIZABETH BOWEN

The following statements are actual quotes from real adversaries within the field of education. They are all statements heard by the school leaders who shared their stories for this book:

- *"I've been in the district longer than you have."*
- *"I deserved that promotion (not you)."*
- *"You didn't do half of what I did last year as a principal."*
- *"You've only been doing this for one year (which isn't close to being long enough)."*
- *"You are not qualified."*
- *"You don't look like a leader, sound like a leader, or act like a leader."*
- *"You do not know these people like I do. I grew up here."*
- *"You've never had any proven success in this area."*
- *"You are nothing like our previous leader."*

These statements drip with jealousy. One of the most common human emotions fueling adversaries is that they are simply *jealous*. Jealous of you. Jealous of not being in the seat you are in. Jealous for not having the opportunities you have. Jealous that coworkers get along with you socially. Jealous of being alone. Jealous of your life outside of work. Maybe even just jealous of your credentials. Sometimes, jealousy breeds regret. So in an effort to land a pitch on your dunk tank target, your adversaries might really be saying to themselves: "I wish I could get my bachelor's degree," or "If only I saved up some money to purchase the house that I wanted, I could be closer to the office too."

The hardest part of the leadership dunk tank is getting past thinking that it's about you. See, it's not *really* about you. It's about *them*; and your adversaries' jealousy is an ugly emotion. It is a rotten spirit. Negative. Crippling. Disease-spreading. So recognize that it exists and don't make it about you—however personal things might seem or become.

REVENGE

> *Before you embark on a journey of revenge, dig two graves.*
> **—CONFUCIUS**

Tonya Rivera, an assistant superintendent for human resources in a large urban school district in Texas, feels waves of revenge crushing her each day when she walks into work:

> *I get up in the morning and think, 'Here we go again.' I've started getting my résumé ready because my time will come. It is inevitable. Sick, but inevitable. I have so much anxiety that my Xanax prescription is already empty and I can't get a refill for another week. All because I recommended the termination of an underperforming science teacher who just so happens to be a relative of our board vice president. Lucky me. I have to do what's right, though, and keeping this teacher around kids is not right. I was hired to do a job and terminating employees is part of HR. I know that I'm doing the right thing. But you*

should see the crap that the VP puts me through. There is a nasty rumor floating around that I'm the superintendent's girlfriend. I wonder where that rumor started. Part of that rumor is that they have video footage of me coming out of his office half-naked. Such a lie. Really, it's slander, but what can I do? My superintendent is in the same boat because he supported my decision and it was his recommendation to place this teacher on leave pending a further investigation for bullying students. We're both on the outs. This sucks. I can't believe the politics involved in education. My friends don't even believe how crazy it is. They're like, 'It's school for kids. Isn't it [your job] to do what you can do to help kids learn?' Well, what I do will help to keep kids safe. HR stinks sometimes. You can't win.

—TONYA RIVERA,
ASSISTANT SUPERINTENDENT, TEXAS

Here, Tonya describes a volatile situation that became harshly adversarial, all because she was doing her job. We started with the concept of jealousy because it is the most common human emotion that breeds discontent and leads to dunk tank intentions. But revenge is often at the heart of the messiest dunk tanks out there. Consider these underlying topics as emotional driving forces under the guise of revenge:

- *"You fired my brother."*
- *"You didn't care that I was out on sick leave; you just assumed I was faking it."*
- *"You negotiated our vacation time out of our contract because you think that the principals have it too good."*
- *"My supervisor is going to learn about how awful you are because of your personal life problems and pitfalls."*

- *"You will never get away with doing that."*
- *"It is not Christian to do that."*
- *"You are not transparent."*
- *"You are friends with the wrong people."*
- *"You are a top-down leader and no one will follow you. You make decisions in a vacuum and, for that reason, we are going to get rid of you."*

The list could go on. Your adversary's life events have established standards or a deeply rooted belief system that convinces them it is justifiable to harm others when they feel as if they are being attacked.

For instance, when an adversary justifies bad behavior with the excuse of "You fired my brother!" what they are really saying is you attacked their underlying belief system of "Never, ever mess with family." The example of "You are not transparent" reveals an underlying belief system of paranoia (*unhealthy* paranoia) that says, "I do not trust you (or maybe anyone)." You can easily see how the other examples also have underlying belief systems, such as the following:

- Standards for being a sensitive and caring leader (if you don't act a certain way at a certain time).
- Standards for measuring moral character (These are often measured by the wrong people—you know the ones. They're the ones who run rampant with a pad of paper and a pen jotting down anything they can in order to judge others.)
- Standards for not being allowed to make a mistake (because you are a leader held to a higher standard)
- Standards for monetary rewards or beliefs about what should be owed to your adversaries

- Standards for measuring how you include others in your leadership plans

Once you recognize the type of revenge that exists, you can easily identify the underlying belief system that governs hateful emotions. Revenge is often the most toxic human emotion because it couples with an active charge against you rather than a passive thought that will be easily forgotten. Revenge is when emotions cross over into action, and it is when those hurtful interactions really begin to *feel* personal.

CONNECTIVITY OR ASSOCIATION

THINK.
Think about your appearance,
associations, actions,
ambitions, accomplishment.
—THOMAS WATSON

Although your personal connections and work associations are not emotions, the need to associate and connect with people can be emotional drivers. Connectivity or association may be the driving forces that cause your adversaries to become jealous—or even worse, take revenge. Earlier in this chapter, you read Russ Peterson's story. Read over these three statements which pertain to his dunk tank situation:

- *"You were hired by the past superintendent (who was a jerk)."*

- *"My cousin knows you from your previous district (and she hates you)."*

- *"You must know someone on the board (because you would have never gotten this job on your own)."*

This is a classic list of "guilty-by-association" labels. If an outgoing superintendent (who was hated throughout the organization) hired you to be the chief of staff, you too might be hated because you are "just like him or her" (even if you are nothing like the former leader). This is how Russ is portrayed by his adversaries.

This guilty-by-association mindset is extremely toxic. The school board doesn't know the real Russ, the chemistry teacher Russ, or Russ the difference-maker. And they aren't interested in getting to know him. But they want him out. Different than pure revenge, guilty-by-association victims haven't *done* anything to trigger an emotional response. They are often positive and dynamic leaders who have been unfairly and inaccurately labeled.

Unhealthy paranoia is related to notions of connectivity and, in this regard, connectivity can either work for you or against you based on the reputations of those with whom you are (or were) previously connected.

Adversaries have a knack for watching for connections—or the appearance of a connection. When this emotional driver has taken over your adversary, you may not even know that a guilty-by-association mindset is the root cause until looking back in retrospect. Putting the puzzle pieces together may take time.

Francesca Benevides experienced this firsthand. She was not able to realize she was in the middle of a guilty-by-association situation until reflecting back on a series of events.

I knew that there was a reason that my boss was treating me differently. She didn't look at me the same or interact with me the same. She started questioning everything I did while tracking my calendar. I knew a switch had been flipped; I went from the star player to a bottom performer, practically overnight.

Throughout the following weeks, I did everything possible to increase dialogue and positively interact with everyone, to no avail. I didn't know what I had done wrong. It was clear that our healthy working relationship was obliterated. I had no clue what caused the 180-degree turn.

I knew that she didn't like working with women, and I knew she had a vengeful reputation, but I had never encountered anything but praise from her. After all, I had worked alongside her for a year as a high performer proving my added value to the organization and my personal investment in student achievement.

One day, she approached me and told me that she heard I went to lunch with another employee and she didn't know about it. I shared that we had an agreement that as long as it was on our shared calendar, then it wasn't an issue. I assured her that I had followed that protocol and notified those in the office before I even left for lunch. She agreed that I had followed the expectation and immediately ended the conversation.

It wasn't until many weeks later that I realized it wasn't the fact that I went to lunch that bothered her—it was the person with whom I went to lunch that was the problem. Later, I found out that my colleague and lunch partner had previously confronted human resources with an issue, and clearly they didn't like it. The fact that I was associated with her at lunch implied that I would also cause confrontation and be a problem in the future, just as she was to them. How was I supposed to know that being friends with somebody would automatically place me on their hit list?

—FRANCESCA BENEVIDES,
TEACHER MENTOR, COLORADO

Unfair? Yes. A lose-lose situation? Yes. Any possible way to defend her own honor? Probably not. Hard to change your adversaries' perceptions of you? Sometimes.

The next two human emotions are not as toxic or dramatic as jealousy, revenge, and connectivity or association. However, they can make your life pretty miserable if your adversaries continue to use them against you.

SKEPTICISM AND VALIDITY

Absence of proof is not proof of absence.
—MICHAEL CRICHTON

Along the lines of jealousy, the "I know better than you" attitude is prevalent in schools. Your adversaries might exhibit skepticism toward your qualifications, judgment, or ability to do your job or lead others. Sometimes, you might be unfairly characterized: "He doesn't look like a strong leader," "He's ugly," or "She seems like a Miss-know-it-all."

Skepticism is very closely linked to validity issues of you being a leader, but validity has more do to with someone questioning your preparedness or qualifications: "I have my Ph.D. and you only have a master's degree," or "He spent only six months as an interim principal and winds up getting the promotion?" are just two examples.

Or as in Kaisha's story below, your adversaries might be "one-uppers."

> *My curriculum director's meetings were always about him, not the content on our agenda. It was a running joke between the other coaches and me. So we would all secretly make tally marks on the bottom of our agenda during Hank's meetings. It seemed to be the only thing we had control over.*
>
> *Hank continuously one-upped nearly every comment, whether it was about vacation, the kind of car he drives, his kids, etc. We turned it into a game by throwing out silly topics that would be used as bait just to see if he would one-up everyone in the room. Sure enough and right on cue, the one-upping comments would fall into play, and the tally marks began.*
>
> *I commented that I had gone to the community pool with my kids, and he had to comment that he took his kids to a Wet-n-Wild water park. Another colleague commented that she went to dinner at an Italian restaurant, and he commented that he went to an even more expensive restaurant where the entreés were fifty dollars or more. Another colleague talked about staying up all night because her child had been getting a cold, and then we had to listen to him talk for the next fifteen minutes about every medical condition his kids ever had.*
>
> *It was all about him, not the meeting topic, not leading educators, not the organization.*
>
> —KAISHA WILLIAMS,
> INSTRUCTIONAL COACH, MINNESOTA

This director was a know-it-all and very jealous person who had a constant need to be validated, which stemmed from his childhood and family pressure to be more like others. He had constantly been compared to his brother and cousins. He had a need to be recognized as better than others:

> *"Some leaders seem to drain intelligence and capability out of people around them. Their focus on their own intelligence and their own resolve to be the smartest person in the room had a diminishing effect on everyone else. For them to look smart, other people had to end up looking dumb. When they walked into a room, the IQ dropped, and the length of the meeting doubled. Other people's ideas suffocated and died in their presence and the flow of intelligence came to an abrupt halt around them. Around these leaders, intelligence flowed only one way: 'downward, from him to them.'"*[2]

One-uppers have a need to constantly outplay their colleagues to ensure that they are always on top. The assumption from the perspective of a one-upping perpetrator is that they are still in control, more qualified than you, and know more than you, and this brings them a comforting sense of validation. The reality is that they are more insecure than you, need constant validation of success, are skeptical of you and your relationships, and are jealous people who cannot enjoy others' successes.

2   Wiseman, Liz. *Multipliers: How the Best Leaders Make Everyone Smarter.* New York: Harper Collins, 2010.

DISCRIMINATION, RACISM, AND NEPOTISM

Life is unfair.
—JOHN F. KENNEDY

Even though our constantly changing, politically correct society frowns upon discrimination and racism today, these attitudes still exist and, despicably, are still used as platforms by some adversaries. The egregiousness of the following statements should send a chill up your spine, but we didn't make them up. Incredibly, our pool of school leaders were on the receiving end of these demeaning comments:

- *"You are a woman (and I don't follow women)."*
- *"You don't attend my church or believe in my God."*
- *"You just moved here; you are an outsider—an alien—who has no right to be here."*
- *"You are way too young to be my boss. I'm old enough to be your father."*
- *"You aren't part of the good old boys' club."*
- *"We've never had a white principal here before."*
- *"Our first black supervisor was a failure. Well, we all know not to hire them again."*

Feelings of hatred or mistrust that are rooted in discrimination and racism create the most difficult forms of adversarial battle conditions to fight. Often established by life experiences or upbringing, these attitudes are almost impossible to remediate.

If your adversary holds a prejudiced view, you will always be defined by your color, age, sex, religion, ethnicity, or any other trait that differs from their own—regardless of the good things you do. Their viewpoint will weigh you down like cement shoes in the dunk tank. And the unfortunate thing is that you may be the only person who can see what is happening since bigots rarely state their beliefs publically—for obvious reasons. So even if they never say what's on their mind, you will feel their silent, unreasonable hatred for you.

Equally as abhorrent is reverse discrimination, something one of our colleagues perpetrated. A white female school district executive we know misused her power by failing to confront two low-performing black employees. Instead, she gave one of these two black employees special treatment and accommodations and, in exchange, that employee acted as the executive's personal informant, providing her with regular "internal intelligence" on the school where he worked. She heralded the other black employee as a positive change agent, even though his lackluster job performance proved otherwise. Because she was Caucasian and they were black, she looked the other way rather than address their performance—even though she knew their job performance was low, their relationships were weak, and they abused the educational system with personalized motives to gain more money, perks, and glory. Interestingly, this same executive saw other white women in her age group as targets and did not hesitate to bully, intimidate, and harass them over the smallest infraction or rumor.

Another form of inequality is nepotism, a form of partisanship. It is inevitable that family members and friends working for someone in a position of power and influence receive preferential treatment. How many of us wouldn't want to hire people we like and trust to do good work just because they are nepotistic allies? Working with friends and family members can be a good thing, but it can also cause huge issues in the workplace—issues that are too taboo to mention. Anyone who has worked in an environment of nepotism knows that the quickest way to end a career is to acknowledge that favoritism exists. The following scenario is rife with inequality and demonstrates a horrendous level of nepotism that existed because the assistant superintendent had various interconnected ally groups in place and felt invincible:

Damion worked in the district for more than twenty-five years as a classroom teacher and, over time, was promoted within the district. Ultimately, he landed the position of assistant superintendent in my school district. He felt a sense of entitlement since he was one of the longest standing members within the district. He truly believed he could do what he wanted, to whom he wanted, and when he wanted. He felt untouchable and acted as if he ruled this dark empire with an iron fist and was immune to the rules set for the organization.

The trouble started out small. He put his mother, brother, and cousin on payroll as district "contractors." After all, Damion—an inner-city Detroit-raised guy—had found success and was now sharing the wealth with his family, even if it meant abusing taxpayer dollars. For him, hiring his friends and family members was an act of self-preservation and a way to spread the wealth. Contractors couldn't earn in excess of what was approved by the business office, but Damion was in complete control of signing off on their time cards and approving payment; and it didn't hurt that he was best friends with the human resources director.

His family members were allowed to work from home or on the weekends. There was even a time when his cousin was working at the district office, and Damion flipped her the keys to his Mercedes and asked her to go run his Benz through the wash. It was second nature for him to allow personal errands during work hours, and he did this without hesitation.

Damion was also a big partier, and he developed personal relationships with people in the office as he partied outside of work. His previous administrative assistant, who was also a close personal friend, had a brother-in-law who had just retired but was still in need of a side job. Even though he wasn't qualified to do the job, Damion hired him.

As time went on, another opening became available for a position in one of his departments. He shared with me that they had been hanging out one evening after work, got to talking with the bartender, and they both really liked him. They hit it off and Damion smirked, "You really need to come work for me." Even though he was not qualified for the job, he hired the bartender for a full-time position in the district simply because he had the same "vibe" as them.

Later in the school-year, a secretary in one of his other departments was "mysteriously" fired and, within weeks, Damion's brother was hired as the new, full-time administrative assistant. It would have been a conflict of interest for his brother to work directly for him, so he layered him in another department under one of the directors.

He also had a childhood friend who was in need of a job. Damion's friend had fallen on hard times and really needed the money to help pay for her son's college tuition, so he pulled the bartender he had just hired into his office and said, "I'm not demoting you. I'm actually giving you more money, but I am going to need to change your title and move you over to another department. I know it feels like a demotion, but it really isn't. You'll actually be doing the same type of work, and you will be getting a raise." He did, in fact, demote his title in order to bring his friend on board at a higher rate of pay and with a higher title. This was necessary in order to disguise an appropriate "trans-action" with the school board so it would get approved. His friend was not qualified, nor did he have the expe-rience to justify doing the job [correctly]. His motive was simple: he wanted to help his friend.

Over time, things started to unravel in several of his departments because Damion was rarely at work; he needed someone in the district office to be his eyes and ears and keep things going. So he called up a former colleague who was already retired (a drinking buddy) and hired him in an administrative role overseeing those various departments.

—HEIDI JACOBI,
ADMINISTRATIVE SECRETARY, IDAHO

Damion hired his mother, brother, cousin, secretary's broth-er-in-law, bartender, childhood friend, and a former drinking buddy, all in less than a two-year span. If you weren't a friend or part of his family, you were intentionally discriminated against.

They say truth is stranger than fiction and, in this case, it is. This example seems outlandish and impossible, but it really hap-pened and, yes, it happened in the field of education. You see, Damion surrounded himself with an army of people who would protect his misbehavior and look past his inability to lead at the executive level. Any outsider walking into this situation would be an immediate target of the school leader's dunk tank. And yet, he wasn't out to hurt anyone specifically; rather, he wanted to hire all of his friends and family members who needed jobs. He didn't start out trying to ruin anyone; he just wanted to help his allies and surround himself with a safety zone. He had good intentions of helping out his family and friends; he just forgot about all the people he hurt along the way. Those who worked for Damion learned that the only way to navigate through an organization saturated with nepotism was to treat everyone connected to the leader with the greatest respect and congeniality.

BEING HELD ACCOUNTABLE

Accountability breeds response-ability.
—**Stephen R. Covey**

You might have heard saying, "If you poke the bear, you might get bit." Those who do not perform well within your organizations or institutions may try to simply "bite you" if you desire to move them toward greater productivity, greater success, and greater accountability than ever before. However, education is becoming more accountable each day through federal and state policy decision-making. Holding people accountable may induce strong emotions. Accountability can also fuel preexisting, negative emotional responses.

While managing is part of leading, we are often faced with situations where poor-quality work is brought to our attention, and then it is up to us to either ignore the new-found information or address it head on. Consider what Natasha Evans, a middle school principal, recently dealt with when evaluating a social studies teacher who also happened to be the teacher union vice president:

I had to evaluate Jessie. I mean, oh my God . . . I sometimes feel like the union protects the weak. I know it's not fair to think that, so I put my money where my mouth was and carried out all of Jessie's annual evaluations and walk-throughs. Jessie received three substandard evaluations and I didn't even receive her end-of-the-year portfolio. So I had to put Jessie on an improvement plan.

Geez . . . you should have been a fly on the wall during that meeting. She started screaming at me that I was retaliating against the union because they were in contract negotiations with the district. Holy smokes . . . it was a meeting that went awry. So all of a sudden, the district gets a human rights notice of claim that I was treating Jessie unfairly because she was black.

That was the icing on the cake. I can't improve teachers who don't want to improve. Some of them just fight and battle. The handcuffs came off. Now, it's all-out war. Why? Because of a poor-quality teacher. Give me a break.

—NATASHA EVANS,
MIDDLE SCHOOL PRINCIPAL, LOUISIANA

Leaders *must* address poor behavior and low productivity. No matter how nice we try to be or how strategic we are with getting others to engage or comply, we still might get "bitten."

Holding others accountable can be uncomfortable. It can lead to hard feelings for those whom we must hold accountable. But almost always, the "bite" might be a form of revenge stemming from *fear*. Here, Jessie might fear so many things: being seen as *inferior* among her peers or losing her job. These fears elicit a fight-or-flight response and, in this case, Jessie decided to fight.

ENTITLEMENT

*You have to do your own
growing no matter how tall
your grandfather was.*
—Abraham Lincoln

While some adversaries exhibit noticeable negative behaviors, other adversaries may appear happy-go-lucky and upbeat. These are the people who believe that they inherently deserve special treatment or privileges of some kind. In the narrative below, Augustus Lucas, a professional development coordinator from New York, shares his experience of dealing with an entitled adversary:

> *I had known her in my past school district, and I was her instructional coach for several years. During my time working with Leesha, I really saw her flourish and grow. When I first worked with her, she just wanted to be friends with her students and party with her fellow teachers. I didn't really have a leadership presence at that time. I was still learning and I still am.*
>
> *Leesha was the life of the party. She loved kids and really knew math content; to me, those were key ingredients to building a leader. Over the course of time, I helped her plan and lead math leadership team meetings, plan for observations, and even team up with some professional-development learning communities.*
>
> *She was very receptive to my mentoring her. She was moving forward and showing tremendous growth. One day, Leesha came to me and asked me if I would fill out*

an application for a National Excellence in Teaching Award nomination form. Of course, I wanted to see her succeed, learn, and grow.

Over the next couple of months, we worked before and after school to complete the application together. I even helped her with her National Board portfolios and attaining another award. To make a long story short, she won and flew to Washington, D.C. to receive the prestigious educational award while she obtained her National Board Certification and other additional state-level awards. She spent her prep hours in my room, and we had many insightful conversations about math practices, math content, student data, and research. I invested a LOT of time in her and saw the fruits of my labor as she grew and flourished into a respected math leader on our campus.

The following year, I was hired as a professional development coordinator in a neighboring school district. I stayed in touch with Leesha throughout the year, both socially and professionally. At the end of the year, I knew we had a math specialist position available, and I couldn't think of a better fit than Leesha. We worked well together; she was in it for kids, so I told her that she should apply. She applied for the position and nailed the interview. I was very proud of her, and we hired her as a math specialist.

I knew there were politics in my district, and I wanted to set her up for success. I organized all of her materials, put important documents in three ring binders, and made an online folder with all of our files for quick access. I wanted to ensure her success. She was thankful and eager to start.

A couple weeks later, I noticed that she was gathering [vertical and horizontal] allies. She gathered them very quickly and from people in high positions. In the weeks to come, I saw her work ethic wane and watched as her *desire to do the right thing flew out the window. She had rallied her new-found allies and leveraged them to her advantage. She wasn't in the office; she was out and about taking long lunches, going to professional-development seminars out of state and hobnobbing around like she was in charge of the entire district.*

I couldn't believe my eyes. It was a flashback to her behaviors that first year when she was befriending her students and partying with her colleagues. She felt as if she had arrived and deserved the freedom to not work hard any longer.

She avoided contact with me and actually started pitting people against me. I have never felt more used and taken advantage of in my entire career. In retrospect, I was being used the entire time. I could pinpoint behavior patterns where she used people and once she got what she needed out of them, she moved on and ditched them. I just didn't see it at the time because I was trying to stay positive and have good intentions.

I had no indication that her motives were going to become corrupt. I was just one person in her path to help her get the titles that she wanted. She felt entitled to these new titles and awards, and I had enabled the behavior all along without realizing it. I still wouldn't change my behaviors; I will continue to serve and help others grow. But I was more than disappointed to have a friend turn into an adversary just because she felt a sense of entitlement.

—Augustus Lucas,
PD Coordinator, New York

Augustus felt duped. What started out as a mentoring relationship quickly turned out to be adversarial. When educators rise to new levels of leadership, one of the most common human emotions is entitlement. Having discussions about entitlement with those whom we mentor or guide through the educational leadership system is one way to decrease the likelihood that our mentees or colleagues will one day become our adversaries.

EGO AND POWER

More the knowledge, lesser the ego.
Lesser the knowledge, more the ego.
—ALBERT EINSTEIN

Ego and the need for power are emotional driving forces that can create formidable adversaries. Some adversaries possess the need to feel important. They are driven by a desire for recognition or control, and they are willing to step on anyone in order to get it.

Your own mental perception of yourself defines your ego. This is known as your mental design. The trouble comes when a person's sense of identity is overinflated or wrapped up in a sense of entitlement. The behaviors exhibited as a result of big egos or an intense desire for power are oftentimes irrational and unpredictable, and can be demanding on others. Consider this story from Calista Ocampo, a curriculum and instruction director, who had to deal with his boss's ego and drive for power:

> *I was actually really excited for our new chief of aca-*
> *demics, Simone. She had a strong reputation, a deco-*
> *rated educational past history of accomplishments, and*
> *seemed highly knowledgeable. I had even attended mul-*
> *tiple trainings that she facilitated as a consultant while*

working in another district. She was highly regarded, and we felt lucky to have her on our team. I later learned that people aren't always what they seem. We had been working on curriculum maps for months with the new adoption of the Common Core standards. We had deconstructed the standards, addressed misconceptions, created essential questions and hyperlinks to online resources, and carried out the whole kit-and-caboodle of one-stop shopping for our teachers.

I can remember multiple times when Simone would ask to look at our curriculum maps during a meeting; she would strike through multiple sections of the texts and instruct us to eliminate them, circle other areas and tell us to modify them, and highlight other areas and tell us to move them. She was highly critical of what we had created. My colleague and I interjected thoughts regarding our research, reasoning, and general philosophy. As we attempted to defend why things should be where they were, she just shook her head, pointed to the doorway, and told us to go fix it [the structure of the document, both literally and figuratively]. We spent hours revising the K–8 documents and working overtime to meet her short revision deadlines.

In our next scheduled meeting, we presented the revisions, only to watch her make a bright red carat indicating that we needed to insert the information back into what we had previously deleted and move the material back to its original position. Her argument was the same exact argument that we gave her in the first meeting while defending why things should stay in their current places. She was flexing her power and feeding her ego so that the final drafts of the curriculum maps would seem to have stemmed from her. Simone's drive for power and control slowed down our organization—all for the sake of her ego. Months later, when I got to know her better, she told me that she would study the night before delivering any PD because she would try her hardest to look like the expert when, in reality, she had learned it the night before and was just "winging it." Her words exactly. This was the moment I knew her ego was covering up for her lack of knowledge.

—CALISTA OCAMPO,
CURRICULUM AND INSTRUCTION DIRECTOR, WEST VIRGINIA

It is easy to put on a façade for a two-hour professional development session with people you have never met and probably will never see again. It is another thing to work and lead people on a day-to-day basis while exhibiting leadership qualities, strong content knowledge, and positive interpersonal relationships. Simone was hiding her incompetence and lack of knowledge behind the mask of ego and power.

FEAR

*A man's doubts and fears
are his own worst enemies.*
—WILLIAM WRIGLEY JR.

Issues of jealousy, revenge, connectivity, skepticism, validity, discrimination, racism, and inequality can often all stem from one central human condition: fear. Yes, you got it: fear. Fear of the unknown. Fear of failure. Fear of the end result. Debilitating, anxiety-inducing fear. You see, your adversaries are willing to not only throw a fast pitch dead on target to dunk tank you, but they may even be willing to reach in and hold you under water in order to fight against your leadership pursuits. For those of you who may have used negative emotions as a protective mechanism to counterattack this type of situation, you may now find yourself in a fight-or-flight response decision-making system. To prevent a negative, knee-jerk counter-response, you must be equipped and able to recognize how your adversaries will react to your daily leadership.

Fear sustains feelings of inadequacy and poor self-esteem as well as the unwarranted protection of something or someone when there is no rational reason to do so. Adversaries will protect the weak, support the squeaky wheels, or condone terrible behaviors. You may have noticed tactics, such as finger pointing and loud voices (as a form of bullying), that are meant to cover up fear. And those fears could be about anything: their own failure, not climbing the district organizational chart, not being able to pay the bills, or losing. You name it.

You see, your adversaries will work against you because they are at war. They see *everything* as a win-lose situation. The strong will win; the weak will lose. And they are out to prove weakness in you—even though they are the weaker ones.

EMOTIONS MOVE US

Although we have provided examples of emotional driving forces, you may never *really* know what fuels your adversaries' actions. In some cases, their behavior or words might make the driving emotion obvious. But it is unlikely that your adversaries will ever come right out and say, "I'm jealous of you," or "I am racist." But we hope we have helped you establish a framework to better understand emotional forces so you can separate your emotions from the conflict with your adversary. Understanding that their behavior is about them—and not about you—will help you determine what is in your control and what is out of your control.

Additionally, if you can think of your adversary as just that—an adversary—rather than an enemy, you may be able to be more understanding of (yet not accepting or permissive of) their behavior—especially when you remember that emotions drive all of us. That one bit of knowledge may even make you more inclined to attempt to bridge the waters between you and your adversary.

The Latin root of the word *emotion* means *to move*. Whenever you feel an emotion, you are automatically moved to do something—cry, laugh, yell, or even scream. Emotional maturity is what helps you decide whether or not it is appropriate to *act* on your emotions.

The emotions that motivate troublesome behaviors are those that make us feel vulnerable and devalued. Some examples are guilt, shame, and anxiety. For some people, the knee-jerk response to those feelings is to try to feel more powerful by devaluing others (expressing the common human emotions of anger, resentment, envy, or jealousy). Others respond to negative emotions by overreacting, overworking, or drinking too much. In some cases, the person's emotional system can become narrow, rigid, and weak, leading to anxiety and depression.

Personally, we have tried and failed to bridge the waters with our adversaries. They were working from highly revengeful platforms. The adversarial conditions we walked into had been in the works for years before we even arrived at our own leadership positions. It would have been impossible to convince those adversaries that we were good people. So we got thrown into the dunk tank. We had to learn to swim—to do what was right and to do our best, despite the circumstances. Along the way, we had a few opportunities to leave and find healthier and happier leadership positions, but a stubborn attitude and the desire to try to fix all of the ills within an organization ended up wearing us out, both physically and mentally. Eventually, we had to escape the high stress and unbearable conditions.

We say all of that to let you know we understand the emotions you are feeling. We know what it is like to go to work and wonder how your adversary's mood will affect your day. Some days, they leave you alone. Other days, their hurtfulness is unrelenting. How you allow yourself to be moved by your emotions can mean the difference between drowning and surviving.

GETTING DUNKED IS INEVITABLE FOR LEADERS

You may have experienced circumstances similar to those of the leaders whose stories you read in this chapter. If you haven't, just wait. It's coming. Because leadership dunk tanks are *inevitable*. Remember the term "proactive paranoia"? Well, it applies to the reality that no leadership pathway is perfect. In fact, we will go so far as to say *no school leader has had a term or tenure where they didn't face adversarial conditions*—whether they were mild, medium, or unmanageable. No one. And if you come into contact with a leader who tells you life "couldn't be better," they are either lying (because they have a fear of failure) or they are not aware of what is happening around them.

So far, this book may seem awash with "doom and gloom" since our focus has been on the varsity dunk tank troop. But it was important for us to share *why they do what they do* so that we can share with you some insights on how to respond to their tactics. It is essential to understand the emotional driving forces behind your adversaries' motives. Now, when you go head-to-head with any player on the varsity dunk tank team, you will be able to analyze who they are, what drives them to play the game, and then determine ways you can counteract their motives and platforms.

Remember: This isn't about "winning" or "losing"—even though it may feel that way to your adversaries. It isn't about accepting your adversaries' behaviors and tolerating dishonesty and corruption. It is about *you* maintaining *you*.

As you think about the human emotions and reactions of those who surround you every day, one thing is for sure: It is extremely difficult to lead the dozens, hundreds, or even thousands of people within an organization. Even the most beloved leaders face adversarial conditions. That's why we love the quote that opened this chapter.

In its most distilled form, it recognizes that barriers are inevitable. Human emotions will always drive behaviors and actions. When you are focused on doing the right things, others may be stuck on emotions that fuel disengagement and a lack of confidence in your leadership. Your awareness of those emotions is like a pair of dunk tank goggles that allows you to see and avoid potential threats. And that means you have a better chance at staying afloat.

Do what you feel in your heart to be right . . . for you'll be criticized anyway.

—**ELEANOR ROOSEVELT**

CHAPTER 3

TEN ADVERSARIAL TACTICS

The secretary called down to my room over the intercom that Thursday morning: "Excuse me for interrupting your class, Ms. Jackson, but we have a new student for your classroom this morning. Could you please send a student up to the front that can walk him back to class?" Without skipping a beat, I continued taking attendance, checking agendas, redirecting students to their bell-work, and replying to a parent e-mail from that morning. Edward left my class to return with Cody, who resembled Pigpen from the

Peanuts cartoon. His toes protruded from his worn-out, too-small sneakers, his pants were soiled with dirt, and a swirl of dust filled with unidentifiable odors surrounded him like a dust devil. I felt an immediate pit in my stomach; he would require nurturing, love, and help to meet his basic needs before we could even come close to teaching him. My eyes welled up, but I held it in and smiled while welcoming him with a chipper tone.

During my prep period later that day, I found out that Cody had been living behind the Circle K nearly his entire life. He attended kindergarten for half of a year and now landed in my third grade classroom. It was my job to close that two-and-a-half year educational gap. Yeah right, I'd be lucky enough to create a safe environment for him to connect with other kids, let alone work an academic miracle. He was discovered and turned over to Child Protective Services (CPS). He missed his dad, no matter how delinquent he was, because it was his dad and they had survived homelessness, together, for two-and-a-half years. They were a team, he loved him, and now all Cody knew was that they had been torn apart.

I worked closely with the child study team to speed up the process of getting him services. I also worked with his new foster family on communicating strategies and supports. Most of all, I worked to make him feel loved. I provided an outlet for him to love his dad. He couldn't read or write, but he was very intelligent. Each morning, I let him voice-record a sound bite to save for his dad. I had it stored on an iPod and would let him borrow it the next time he would visit his dad. He could play his messages for his dad. This provided a daily connection to what mattered most to Cody: his father.

Over time, with nurturing, love, communication, and support, Cody started to learn, grow, and thrive. He was so smart that he still retained his letter sounds and name recognition all the way from kindergarten. His reading interventions were intense, and he was getting it. He was learning to read! We celebrated him constantly and my students loved him.

After we came back from spring break, my heart was torn open. Cody was no longer on my roster. He was one of my own. I cared about him more than anything that year. I wondered. I worried, and the kids . . . the kids missed him. The class wasn't the same without him. I would never be the same. He taught me more than any in-service training ever could because he taught me about resilience and perseverance.

—CHARMAINE JACKSON,
SUPERINTENDENT OF SCHOOLS, MICHIGAN

Charmaine was an all-star teacher and should be crowned teacher of the universe for her depth of concern and understanding for Cody (and the needs of all of her students). She's one of the good ones and she always will be. Many years have passed since the year she spent learning more about herself through Cody. Charmaine continued impacting students, teachers, and leaders and now serves as a superintendent of schools in Michigan. However, her story took a dark turn when she entered the leader's dunk tank zone.

The decisions you must make as a school leader get progressively harder the higher you climb in your career—especially if you commit to doing what's right. Those difficult decisions can put you in the dunk tank zone when you inadvertently cross someone. In Charmaine's case, the decision was to recommend the termination of an employee. Read on to learn about the experience she had within her school district:

Being superintendent is not easy. My board of education members liked me for the most part, except one member named Sarah. Sarah hated me, and I can understand why even though it doesn't seem really fair. A few years ago, my director of human resources had to fire Jake, an athletic director, because he was sexually harassing one of the coaches. We gave him a few chances to knock it off. He didn't, though. So we had no choice but to terminate his employment, otherwise we would have faced severe financial and legal consequences. Well, Sarah was close friends with Jake, and from the day he was terminated, she sought revenge.

Our Employee Assistance Program was there to help Jake, but he didn't follow through with getting the help that he needed. So I had no choice but to support the termination. The majority of the board supported my recommendation, but from there, it went from bad to ugly, and Sarah, well . . . she basically came after me. I don't mean that she physically came after me, but she made my life a living hell. She did everything in her power to work against me and make me look completely incompetent. I felt like I was suffocating. I couldn't get anything done with a clear mind. The rumors she spread about me were unbearable. The public humiliation that Sarah put me through during my board presentations to the community was insane. I know I had to be a tough leader and deal with adversaries, but c'mon . . . I'm human too and get stressed out like anyone else. Being a superintendent doesn't mean that I stop being a human being with feelings and emotions.

Charmaine's story is not unique. Adversarial conditions like these happen all the time to good-hearted educators. Charmaine understood that leadership would be difficult, but she didn't sign up for warfare conditions. She missed the life and the sense of self-worth she had when she could nurture students like Cody.

Being a school leader can be a very lonely job. The weight of the organization falls on your shoulders, and you face the likelihood of a higher number of adversarial encounters based on the sheer number of people you support. No matter what your position is—academic coach, assistant principal, dean, principal, coordinator, mentor, assistant superintendent, director, superintendent, etc.—you will face adversity. And no one has prepared you for this kind of life. Your college or university program, most likely, did not discuss the dissension and opposition school leaders face because the topic is taboo. Why would they want to scare you out of education? Adversity is inevitable. It is difficult. It is emotional. It is taxing. It may lead you to do things that you normally wouldn't do. It clouds your judgment. It adds a level of stress in your life that you cannot possibly fathom before stepping into a leadership role.

While an array of possible solutions existed for Charmaine, there were not any *quick* solutions. Worse yet, it may have been impossible for her to reclaim her respected reputation from the grips of rumor and gossip. Regardless, she had to try.

Charmaine felt her best option was to gather and present empirical information regarding Jake's termination recommendation to her board members, including Sarah. Even if the board members had fixed mindsets about the situation, she knew that to ignore the claims put forth against her would reinforce the rumors of her ineffectiveness as a leader. Worse, ignoring Jake's behavior would put both her and the district at risk. She had to address Jake's poor behavior, knowing that it was likely impossible to change the misconceptions the board members now had of her. Charmaine felt like she was in a "lose-lose" situation and that the termination recommendation would be the sword her career would die on. Knowing the risks, she chose to do the right thing:

> *I wouldn't change one thing about my decision. I wouldn't change one thing about making sure there was peace in the district. Yep . . . I went through the firing squad over all of this, but what can I say? Rumors and reputations are in the eye of the beholder, I guess. You win some; you lose some. Even though the board did not renew my contract, I'll land on my feet somewhere else. I have to believe that, or they will truly have gotten the best of me.*

While Charmaine did not specify the types of rumors or public humiliation she endured within her original narrative, she told us later that Sarah activated a series of highly calculated rumors about her. Through a partnership with one of Charmaine's assistant superintendents (someone who wanted Charmaine's job), Sarah attained personal information in order to work against Charmaine. Sarah twisted information about Charmaine's private life, failed marriage, and troubled teenager, whom she was raising alone, to fabricate rumors that would reflect poorly on Charmaine. All of this helped Sarah to move her revengeful platform forward—and ultimately led to Charmaine's resignation due to job-related stress.

TACTICS OF THE TRADE

We've spoken to hundreds of school leaders about the tactics their adversaries have used. In the following section, you will learn about the ten tactics that came up time and time again within our discussions with school leaders from coast to coast.

We find it interesting that these tactics are quite common. We invite you to examine any similarities to circumstances that you might be going through or have seen unfold in your school or district.

ADVERSARIAL TACTIC NO. 1: CREATING RUMORS

> *We must set up a strong*
> *present tense against all rumors*
> *of wrath, past and to come.*
> **—RALPH WALDO EMERSON**

They went after me, full barrel. I never thought that being a principal would be like this. I had to move a few teachers around into different grade levels at my school because of a few retirements that took place the previous year. I met with the union, the grade-level teams, and I even ran my plans past the superintendent. When I met with the teachers, I could feel some of them cutting me open with their eyes. Their glares spooked me. A few teachers came in to see me privately and asked me to reconsider my grade-level assignments. I didn't really hear any good reasons why I should change things to suit the individual likes of only a few teachers. They were all certified to teach K–6. Some of them moved from third grade to fourth grade. These were good teachers. Yet they felt panicked.

Something was just so odd to me about the whole thing. A few of them had to change their classroom locations so they would be on the first floor in our primary wing instead of upstairs with our intermediate grades. One teacher slammed my door on the way out. At least I had summer vacation to breathe, or so I thought. After a few weeks, when things quieted down, I received a flurry of parent letters and complaints about the new grade-level changes. It started out as one or two letters, but then it turned into fifty . . . sixty . . . I couldn't believe it. It was insane. I have no proof who led this stand against me. I thought I was just making some changes to help kids. To help us grow.

Then I received an e-mail from a strange e-mail address that I had never seen before. A Gmail address. It simply had one web link attached to it. Stupid me, I clicked on it. It took me to a blog that had pictures of me on it with hateful messages. Rumors about me being married to another woman. Pictures of my daughter. I felt sick to my stomach. I couldn't believe my eyes. I couldn't believe that this was happening all because I switched a few grade level teachers around?

—Amelia Sinha,
Principal, Georgia

While the act of changing some grade-level assignments seems to be a simple leadership decision, Amelia was faced with adversarial conditions even though she couldn't pin anything on her teachers. She had no proof of who was spreading the rumors. Nevertheless, her experiences were real and troubling.

Rumors—physical or sexual rumors, rumors about mental competency, career reputation rumors, and other types of career-bashing rumors—are created and spread in many school settings across the nation. While the perpetrators hide behind an anonymous Gmail account, the victim's reputation is irreparably damaged.

When faced with rumors, the goal is to stay in the mindset of "sticks and stones will break my bones but names will never hurt me." Yet that's easier said than done. Technology makes it easy for adversaries to spread damaging information. Anyone can create a Gmail account or anonymous blog. Anyone can place (almost) anything they want on a blog and, using search engine optimization, make those negative, hurtful claims rise to the top of a Google search. That kind of false digital footprint may end up following the victims when they try to move on to a new leadership position. So not only will current peers and employers see the search results, those rumors will be seen by future hiring officials as well.

The real problem is not technology or the fact that you can try your best to not let rumors affect you. The real issue is that school leaders have not been prepared to handle extreme adversarial conditions.

In this case, Amelia was under attack. She faced an army of upset parents and a negative, hurtful digital footprint that would follow her wherever she went. Even if someone were wise enough to dismiss the rumors and realize that it was all a bunch of hateful nonsense, the mere existence of those rumors could create questions or skepticism in the minds of hiring officials, which could make leaders like Amelia look like damaged goods.

The adversarial tool of spreading rumors and creating a false, negative digital footprint is a real problem. Even if you are able to emotionally dismiss them, the risk is that others might very well believe the rumors. What about the unrest, turmoil, and stress these adversarial conditions create? What if the rumors start to show up during meetings, parent group forums, and the like? What will you do to stand tall and deal with it? What will you do if your loved ones are made to look foolish and your credibility in the community diminishes? Ignore it? Perhaps. Confront it head on? Maybe. Will you be able to handle the stress? It's impossible to say until it happens.

It is easy to say, "I'd never let any of that garbage get the best of me." But we are all human. We all have feelings. We all deal with things differently. We all truly want to be liked, even if we don't want to admit it.

For Amelia, completing another year at her school was difficult. Allegations of domestic violence and rumors that she beat her child started to surface all over her small Georgian community. Amelia started to drink more and more each night after her thirteen-hour work days. Amelia was hospitalized for back pain on three occasions and later became dependent on her pain medication. In the end, the stress proved too much to bear. Amelia is no longer a principal. She and her daughter moved back to her hometown to live with her mother. We can't judge Amelia for how she tried to cope with the hatred. All we can do is learn from her story and think about proactive ways to try to prevail in our careers even when others want to see us drown.

Amelia is prevailing today. She recently got married to a police chief in northern California, and she now enjoys her life as a stay-at-home mom even though she misses working in the field of education. She regularly volunteers at her daughter's school and at church. She sought help for her drug and alcohol addictions and now leads workshops for parents to explain the toll that painkillers and alcohol can have on one's life. Her impact on society and the legacy of helping others is her new victory, and no one can ever take that away from her.

ADVERSARIAL TACTIC NO. 2: SLOWING DOWN THE ORGANIZATION

> *Stern accuracy in inquiring,*
> *bold imagination in describing,*
> *these are the cogs on which history*
> *soars, flutters, or wobbles.*
> **—THOMAS CARLYLE**

After the retirement of the human resources director and district treasurer, there was more work to be done by the superintendent and me. I'm not allergic to work. Don't get me wrong. But when we have loads of litigation going on against us from a principal and teacher who are suing us, life can be miserable for us around here, indeed. And they know that they are making life miserable for us.

That's the most deranged part of all of this. I actually hate coming in to work now. There is always a new Freedom of Information Laws (FOIL) request on my desk from one of the "demons," as I call them. Or there is a phone message from our lawyer asking us to put together more documents for our defense. See, the thing is, they know that they were wrong by stealing money out of the high school student account. They know that we were keeping track of them. Instead, they seem to be on the offense. And my work is now consumed with FOILs, litigation e-mails, and paperwork related to the division of human rights lawsuits. Give me a break! We placed them on leave and they sue us.

Yeah . . . they are cogs in the wheel, I get it. The squeaky wheels get the grease, right? But c'mon, look at all of the other stuff we could be doing and how it takes away from kids. Litigation stinks. I wish my school business certificate program would have gone over this one for us. All I do is work on this case. It really stinks. Really. I'm not sure how much longer I want to stay here. It is too draining.

—TINA KRAMER,
CHIEF OF BUSINESS AND GRANTS, CALIFORNIA

The adversarial tool of slowing down an organization can come in so many different forms. FOIL provide outlets for potential abuse, demanding e-mail requests, litigation, and more paperwork relative to any or all the above that become daily chores for school leaders everywhere.

Tina is worn out. *Tired.* And her adversaries know it. Her office is short staffed, she has extra work on top of all of her normal duties, and the stress of it all makes Tina want to leave the district. She doesn't feel fulfilled. Who would? This wasn't the job she bargained for, and the litigation is sure to last a while.

Your adversaries will clog the system. This is one of the tools that they use to wage war against an organization or against you personally. While this tool is not exclusive to educational settings, it shows up frequently in schools across the nation. When revengeful adversaries make the job or lifestyle of school leadership completely draining and maddening, the tendency is for school leaders to retreat and seek refuge in other, more peaceful organizations. Here, the dunk tank does not attack us directly, but it makes us scramble for new work elsewhere. Some of us land on our feet and some of us don't.

We have a choice to leave and look for new work, yes. But the reality is, our choice becomes *involuntary* because it isn't really what we want to do. Sam Jenkins, a school superintendent in Minnesota, says it best: "I know how crazy education is. We are dinosaurs. The moment I get a new job, I update my resume knowing that I'll need it (hopefully) later rather than sooner. I know my time in any school district is rented, temporarily." Does Sam have a negative attitude? No. Is Sam an ineffective leader? No. Definitely not.

ADVERSARIAL TACTIC NO. 3: (MIS)USING THE POWER OF INFORMATION

An exaggeration is a truth
that has lost its temper.
—KAHLIL GIBRAN

The use of e-mail in our district has run amuck. The organization is so stirred up every time Sandra sends out information to the teachers about contract negotiations. And of course I don't see the e-mail because administration is not copied in on the correspondences. I get a printed copy from some of the teachers who want to tell us about what is happening out there with contractual matters—especially if it is toxic to the organization. So Sandra always misinterprets the contract. Then the board hears about it and thinks that I am not following the teachers' contract. Then it becomes a big mess in executive session.

The board members like Sandra. They side with her. Some of them are close friends with Sandra. Sandra is just up to no good. Period. She makes my life miserable. I've tried to work with the union leaders to get her to knock it off, but they don't do anything about it, either. I've even sat down with Sandra and her union rep to talk with her (nicely) about coming to her rep or me before she sends out misinformation. That didn't work either. The board, Sandra, and so many others just permit her to ruin the morale in this district.

I'm not sure how much more of this I can take, but I'll tell ya . . . it is wearing on my every nerve. My teachers get upset with me because they think I'm making teachers work past their six class duty assignments or I'm not providing travel time for the traveling teachers. All of it is false and misconstrued. I know Sandra wants me out because I didn't give her friend a job. It is so crazy how so many things here have to do with people not getting a job they want for a friend, relative, or, yes, even a spouse. Well, I look for the best candidate, not just the ones who are perceived to be great because they are homegrown or related to (or friends with) someone in a power position.

—TYRONE PHILLIPS,
SUPERINTENDENT, LOUISIANA

Many of the school leaders we have talked to report that misusing information is a common, powerful adversarial tool. Here, contractual misinterpretations led to multiple grievances within an organization. One might argue that building a trusting organization can resolve any issues even before they become a grievance. That is true. We believe that. However, it is not always possible to rely on trust to resolve issues when dealing with irrational people.

Sometimes grievances are made simply to prove a point. We are not saying that grievances are a bad thing. In fact, grievances are necessary, especially when school leaders ignore contractual obligations. As school leaders, we have a duty to follow our bargaining unit contracts. We should not revise, alter, or delete items from a contract until or unless those particular items are negotiated. We must fulfill our responsibilities as leaders in order to sustain and respect our staff members and their agreements with the district. But fair play requires both sides communicate truthfully and accurately.

ADVERSARIAL TACTIC NO. 4: CREATING UNHEALTHY COMMUNITY PARANOIA

Acting is the perfect idiot's profession.
—KATHARINE HEPBURN

You won't believe the politics in my district. Over technology. Computers! You gotta be kidding me.

I've been in the district for three years. I was hired by a really good superintendent and nice board members. That's why I came. Everything felt right. So, my superintendent retired and the board changed last July. Now it's like that Iron Maiden song, "Run to the Hills." And I'm running.

I was brought in to lead an infrastructure overhaul—a new wired and wireless system that would allow the district to handle a bring-your-own-device philosophy. We wanted to open up our network while still keeping things secure. The company we went with had a higher bid than the one we turned down, but we chose it because it had better testimonials and a better product outlook and outreach for the project specs.

Now I'm under attack from the board because a friend of a few of the board members works for the technology company we didn't hire. Stories about kids being able to surf porn started to circulate around the district and community. It all wasn't true, and I did positive PR events and sent home information, but it didn't matter. Some of my flyers didn't make it home with the kids. My technology night was sparsely attended. So many weird things started happening. Then I found out that my position was going to be abolished at the end of the year!

Board meetings were crazy. Board members grilled me about the perceived problems—issues that weren't problems with our infrastructure at all. When I was being hung out to dry by my superintendent, the board kept firing shots at me, and the crowd clapped every time they came after me.

Now I'm without a job, and I think my reputation went down the drain. All because of what: personal interests in getting the friends of the board members a contract with our district for technology installations? At the same time, one of the accusations was that I had a shady deal with our technology contractor and was getting a kickback. Total fiction. I guess money talks, and when there isn't any money for the personal interests of others, I'm not doing any of the talkin'. All I am left with is walkin'.

—TODD OWENS,
DIRECTOR OF TECHNOLOGY, ARIZONA

Todd faced adversarial conditions that manipulated the community into the following:

- Questioning his professional leadership and judgment
- Creating perceived incompetence
- Creating a smoke screen for hidden agendas while attacking his character
- Creating community unrest through unhealthy paranoia

Furthermore, Todd was faced with unreasonable demands, based on suspicions, when the board directed the superintendent to carry out a forensic study of Todd's laptop and desktop computer. They alleged foul play with his decision-making for going with a different technology contractor. All of this was done using public confrontations, sneak attacks, and unjust public ridicule when applause from the audience was reported in the local newspaper. The board generated unhealthy paranoia as a tactic to remove Todd—and it was successful. All of the documentation in the world wouldn't have saved Todd. The board wanted what they wanted. The superintendent was at the mercy of their actions; he had to comply or risk his job being threatened as well.

ADVERSARIAL TACTIC NO. 5: CREATING SILOS

> *Reality is easy. It's deception*
> *that's the hard work.*
> **—LAURYN HILL**

I felt like I was always the last one to know anything. One afternoon, I was approached by my boss, who was the executive director of school support. He wanted me to create a video for each school showcasing its focus. Assigning STEM, art, leadership, and dual-language were all a lure for a higher student count. Evidently, this was part of the marketing for the upcoming school year. The decision was made last minute to assign a focus to each school within the district. The video would be featured as advertising school choice. The catch was, the videos were due within a week, and I wasn't given any criteria other than to work with the principals.

I knew this was an extremely short timeline to edit multiple videos for multiple schools, so I was really hoping that each school already had a storyboard and footage ready to go. I picked up the phone to talk with one of the principals to collaborate on their focus school commercial. I asked the principal for the criteria of the film and what they already had prepared. This particular principal said that he didn't have any specific criteria that were given to him, but he had a couple ideas of what they wanted to film.

No direction had been given as far as length of the film or consistency in messaging from one school to another; they had free reign. This made my job even harder because not only was I the film editor on a short timeline, I was also now the producer. Later, I happened to be in the curriculum department talking to the director about my predicament, and she rattled off a short list of criteria. She said they had discussed it in their directors' meeting. From this short conversation, I discovered the desired length of the films, the branding focus, and the marketing strategy. The principals had been in a meeting with the executive team and had been asked several weeks prior to meet with their staff and generate a possible focus school idea that they would be interested in piloting for the upcoming school year. They had only batted around ideas.

In short, the principals came up with their focus school topic, the directors understood the video criteria, while the executive team had the vision of what they wanted carried out. Nobody had all the information or really even knew why this had become a crisis to all of us. It took each one of us talking to one another to piece things all together in order to get a clear picture of what the superintendent actually wanted. We found out later that our enrollment was down, and in order to compete with neighboring districts, the executive team had come up with the last-minute, knee-jerk idea of creating focus schools in hopes of attracting more students to the district.

Furthermore, the executive team didn't want me to know about this initiative because they didn't want me to be a part of the collaborative plan. They knew that I am methodical and strategic when planning. They threw this together, last minute, and didn't want me to be a part of the plan so I was left out until the end. They weren't going to give the principals a choice about "if" focus schools were happening or not, only letting them offer a topic. The directors in the teaching and learning department knew how to carry out the plan, but that information wasn't shared with the rest of the stakeholders. The executive team clearly didn't want one group talking to the other group because collectively they could have stood up against the idea altogether. They gave each group their specific piece of information and no more. They didn't want their plan foiled by people talking. They wanted me to be a worker bee with no collaboration. I felt pushed aside and devalued.

—*DIETRICH SULLENS,*
TECHNOLOGY COORDINATOR, OHIO

What Dietrich faced was an intentional top-down silo effect. A silo effect often takes place in an organization where one department doesn't want to share information or ideas with another department. It could be because of competition, control issues, or the intent to make a school leader look bad by making it seem as if he or she has lack of ownership (when in reality they aren't privy to information).

In Dietrich's example, the superintendent had an idea to save enrollment, but she didn't want her plan foiled. She didn't want input from her people, and she didn't want one group talking to another. She simply wanted it done, no questions asked, with no collaboration.

She gave each of the following groups of professionals one separate piece of the overall pie of information:

1. Executive Team: the vision

2. Directors: the criteria and expectations

3. Principals: the topic or focus

4. Technology Specialist: the directive to complete the task

As a result of the lack of communication and short timeline, all stakeholders (except the executive team) were frazzled. The principals worked closely with Dietrich to accomplish the task to the best of their ability even without a clear vision or cultural investment in the project. They worked overtime and on a long holiday weekend in order to meet the short deadline. Upon completion, the videos were uploaded to the district website without the executive team even previewing all of them.

Dietrich shared with us that a big community event was held the next week. Parents were invited to come to the district office to learn about the new focus of each school and to choose a school that best met the needs of their child. During the community event, the superintendent walked around and watched the videos for the first time as they were rolling for the audience and became quickly irritated. Dietrich found out later that the superintendent was furious at some of the comments, content, and over-promising that principals had shared in their videos regarding their school focus. Clearly the superintendent's silo-mentality decreased efficiency, fragmented her people, and created a cultural nightmare. In the end, she transformed her people into unthinking robots that did not produce the outcome that she had expected. Can you imagine how this project may have turned out differently if the superintendent had all stakeholders plan this project together?

CHAPTER 3· TEN ADVERSARIAL TACTICS

ADVERSARIAL TACTIC No. 6: INTENTIONAL OMISSION

Just because something isn't a lie does not mean that it isn't deceptive. A liar knows that he is a liar, but one who speaks mere portions of truth in order to deceive is a craftsman of destruction.

—CRISS JAMI

I was in the position of curriculum specialist. Upon hire, I was told, in multiple settings, that I was so talented and should really be moved into a coordinator position. I was on the "good list" for more than three years. I had a strong reputation and was well regarded throughout the district.

Somewhere along the way, my supervisor heard a rumor about me and decided to believe the second-hand information and retaliated against me because of it. One day, the human resources director and my supervisor sat me down and told me, "We wanted to let you know that next year your position will be moved to another department, because we are opening two coordinator positions. We are so impressed with your talent and leadership skills and would like you to lead our instructional coaches next year and teach them how to do walk-throughs in classrooms like you run, because your communications are phenomenal. Your role would be to work together to lead the coaches. We want you to teach them what you do."

Without hesitation, I thanked them and agreed that it was a great idea to have all the leaders working together in collaboration. They both smiled and looked at each other and were surprised by my response. They looked surprised that I took the news so well. They were taken by surprise because I swallowed their bait without choking on the hook. I called up a close friend and shared the news that I had this upcoming opportunity to be a coordinator. I had planned on resigning at the end of the school year. Now it seemed as though they had retracted the misconceptions they had about me enough to recognize my true talent and leadership. I felt as though I needed to rethink my career path to consider staying on in this new leadership role. I was in such profound shock that they had offered me a promotion, when all along I thought they were out to get me. At the time I just thanked them because I really didn't have a response; I was shocked, but happy. All along I had told my close friends (based on their past interactions with employees) that either they would push me up or push me out. I assumed it would be the latter. I was flattered that they recognized my talent and chose the high road.

The next day I went into my supervisors' office to clarify the information. I let her know that I was surprised by our conversation and flattered that they recognized my good work, so I repeated back what they had said and asked the clarifying question: "When I move over to the other department, am I moving over into a coordinator position?" In a non-engaged, monotone response, while engaged with her phone, she looked up over the top of her glasses as her eyes rolled and responded, "No, you are just moving over there; it's a lateral move."

A mirage. They painted me a mirage.

—Pauline Cranford,
Curriculum Specialist, Oregon

The power of information makes all the difference. Pauline's adversaries worded things in such a way that they didn't want her to think that they were pushing her off to another department, but the reality was they mislead her by not providing all the information. Her boss and the human resources director flexed their power by omission. Intentionally. By adding flattery and omitting information, they flowered things up enough that Pauline should have been happy enough to stay.

When does omission become a lie? How close can you dance on that gray line? Is an omission on the spectrum of lies? Is omission the entry-level version of a lie? Does it become a lie when you actually give a mistruth? Or is it only a lie when there is intention to deliberately hurt the recipient? We would venture to say that if you are omitting information that may sway a person's opinion or judgement, then it is clearly a lie.

This type of behavior was so routine for these particular school leaders that there was no consideration of whether it would positively or negatively impact Pauline; in their estimation, they were simply offering revenge in what they hoped she would receive as a compliment. They were abusing their power by omitting information and intentionally inferring something completely false.

Adversarial Tactic No. 7: Working from the Inside

*Setting people to spy on one another
is not the way to protect freedom.*
—Tommy Douglas

The human resources director in my district had the reputation for being dishonorable. I had heard countless stories about how he had ruined people's reputations and worked to get enough information about people to reprimand them or, even worse, fire them. Even though I knew this was something that people feared and had even seen employees walked out and fired by him, I wasn't worried about it. I knew that I was a hard worker with high ethics. I would just stay out of it and do my job.

One day, I went to an IEP meeting at one of the schools. After the meeting wrapped up, I started chatting with the classroom teacher, and we got to talking about the upcoming school board meeting. We were one of the only districts in the state with a 200-day calendar rather than a 180-day calendar. The school board would be voting on whether they would be reducing the number of calendar days. I shared that I was hopeful that they would reduce it to 180 days because it may help with teacher retention and the high turnover rate. This teacher asked me if I thought that the 200-day calendar was the only reason for the high turnover in our district or if I thought there were additional factors. I shared with her that I thought there were multiple factors, including the instability in curriculum, lack of communication, and lack of supporting professional development. We talked for a few more minutes about how we could make a positive impact on the district if a few things were different. Overall, I left the IEP meeting and the conversation with the teacher feeling helpful and connected.

Less than twenty-four hours later, I was called into my director's office and was told to shut the door and sit down. She stood over me with her arms crossed and asked me why I was out on the campuses spreading rumors about the district office. I assured her that I had no idea what she was talking about. She told me that she had a meeting with the human resources director first thing that morning and she heard that I was talking derogatorily about the school calendar, that we are an awful district with an incredibly high turnover rate, and that the district office doesn't collaborate. Once I heard those details, it triggered me back to the conversation I had with the teacher the day before. Boy, did news travel fast, and boy was the information twisted! Clearly, this teacher had a direct line to the human resources director.

—CHRISTOPHER CLYDE,
SPECIAL EDUCATION TEACHER ON SPECIAL ASSIGNMENT, MAINE

As a rookie to the district, Christopher clearly did not understand the depths of the dunk tank or its underground connections. Later, Christopher shared with us that over the course of the year, he discovered that other employees had experienced similar incidents. One day, a colleague at the district office, a thirteen-year veteran, shared this story with Christopher:

I guess the cat's out of the bag, if you didn't know already, the human resources director has a spy at every campus. Just watch the people who get to go on out-of-town trips and who are signed up to help with district committees. They are all the insiders. They text him all the time and report right back to him, and he actually believes everything they tell him—whether it is substantiated or not.

Just keep your nose clean and know which people to stay
in good with. Just know that anything you tell them will
go straight to him. And let me tell you, you don't want
him on your bad side.

The human resources director and the teachers he had planted at each campus had an unspoken agreement. In return for information, these teachers were given privileges such as approved time off on blackout days, approved professional development trainings, and even requests for equipment and supplies that they couldn't afford. It was a symbiotic agreement from which both parties benefitted. The employees who were willing to go along with this black market of information were, themselves, unethical. They viewed any employee who was willing to stand up for student achievement or call out the real problems needing to be addressed as adversaries. In this case, what was considered good was bad and what was bad was considered good. The moral: Beware those on the inside, because they might not be able to keep the truth straight.

Adversarial Tactic No. 8: Extending (and Bending) Professional Courtesy

> *You may choose to look the other way,*
> *but you can never say again*
> *that you did not know.*
> **—William Wilberforce**

I can't believe that all I got was a little hand slapping. If
it had been anyone else, they would have taken their keys
and fired them on the spot. After they went through my

letter of reprimand for hacking into the district security cameras, we were all laughing and joking. They even told me to go enjoy my two days of unpaid leave and not to worry about anything. We high-fived and hugged it out, and I dodged a big bullet that nobody else would have gotten away with. I know it's because my director likes me and because she hired me. I was her favorite, and she just has always liked me and treated me better than everyone else.

—IAN GLADSTONE,
TECHNOLOGY TECHNICIAN, FLORIDA

Even though Ian's intent was not malicious, he had committed a crime that was grave enough to terminate his employment. He didn't have permission or rights to be logging into the district cameras remotely from home. Ian was offered a professional courtesy when he received the least reprimand possible and was assured that he was still on the inside club and protected.

By title alone, one might assume that extending professional courtesy would be a notable attribute. However, *professional courtesy* is a term often used within the police force when a police officer "looks the other way" when a fellow police officer is caught committing a crime. Even if an officer undeniably broke the law, the crime will not be filed, and the guilty police officer will not face charges. In essence, the infraction would just go away. Within the medical field, extending professional courtesy means offering free or discounted services to friends and family. Although this may be backed by positive intent, medical professionals are not adhering to the laws and guidelines from the Office of the Inspector General (OIG). Unfortunately, we have witnessed many scenarios of extending professional courtesy in the educational field when fueled by adversarial conditions.

Here's what *extending* or *bending* professional courtesy looks like in education:

1. Offering paid overtime to preferred employees while excluding other employees from gaining overtime hours and pay

2. Allowing preferred employees the ability to flex their time while excluding others

3. Allowing preferred employees to log their mileage for pay while excluding others.

4. Allowing preferred employees to lose their iPad, laptop, or cell phone with no reprimand, payback plan, or documented loss

In our journey of writing *Escaping the School Leader's Dunk Tank*, we have heard countless scenarios of professional courtesies being carried out. It happens all the way to the superintendent level.

> *I was hand delivered a letter stating that I must be present for a hearing in human resources based on an investigation and accusation by the chief of academics. Clearly, they didn't have all the facts, nor did they understand the nature of the accusation. During my hearing, I shared additional information that they were unaware of and they said they understood completely. They even stepped out for a minute to deliberate and both came back looking at ease and agreed that I was not at fault. They no longer felt I was guilty, and they told me that they officially downgraded the accusation to a verbal warning. Our school board policy clearly states that if a written*

warning is issued, it is to be served in writing within ten business days of the hearing. So after the tenth business day following the hearing, I felt as though the world had been lifted from my shoulders. I knew that it really was a verbal warning and now the whole situation could finally be put to rest for good.

Not long after the tenth business day had passed, I was served with an informal written warning from the chief of academics to be placed in my file. She slid it across the desk and said, "Here, sign this." I noticed it didn't even have the correct date on it. She was trying to get me to sign a backdated document. I couldn't believe that she was trying to get me to sign a document to cover for missing her own deadline.

I was dumbfounded! I reread the school board policy again, and the next step in the process would be to write an appeal to the superintendent. I was done taking the bullets, trying to defend my honor time and time again, and was finally willing to stand up for myself. I wrote the superintendent a succinct attorney-like letter that stated the terms in the school board policy that had been violated and listed all the factual information from the allegations and situation. Several weeks later, the administrative secretary to the superintendent hand delivered the superintendent's reply. It stated that the school board policy was an approximation and not literal, that life happens, and it was my fault anyway.

—Ramona Vega,
Principal, Oklahoma

Here, the superintendent clearly extended (and bent) professional courtesy to the chief of academics. He looked the other way and avoided reality. He accepted corruption. He didn't want to face the harsh reality that his own organization wasn't playing by the rules. His natural instinct was to push back and cover his tracks. If Ramona had escalated the situation to the school board level, I'm sure that they would have agreed that policy is policy—not an approximation open for interpretation. What extending/bending professional courtesy really means to all organizations and their communities is that inequity, resentment, and distrust of the organization exists. The adversarial tactic of extending/bending professional courtesy is an extension of adversarial tactic No. 7 (Working from the Inside) because it is often carried out from the inside. It is a form of preferential treatment. Extending professional courtesy in education is an inside job that rewards poor behavior and avoids reprimanding employee misconduct, especially if they are part of the inner sanctum.

Adversarial Tactic No. 9: Nepotism

Power doesn't corrupt people;
people corrupt power.
—William Gaddis

I was so excited that I would be getting a data entry specialist to support my department with data and assessment. I had worked so many late nights I couldn't even remember what it looked like to go home and eat dinner with my husband at a normal hour. I wasn't sure who we were getting for this new data entry position. I just knew it was a detail-oriented job that required precision and a strong understanding of spreadsheets and information systems.

Shortly after receiving the news, I happened to be in a meeting with the assistant superintendent of instruction and assessment, sharing the most recent data from our quarterly benchmark assessment. After the meeting, I acknowledged that I was more than grateful to be getting the additional support. I asked when they were going to post the job and when they thought the interviews might begin. The assistant superintendent shared with me that one of the part-time contracted workers that the business office had been using for the past few weeks would just slide into the position temporarily and would begin work on Monday. He shared with me that I should carve out some time and be prepared to begin training her right away. My jaw just about dropped to the floor. He was talking about his cousin that had been coming in to make deliveries and make copies for the mailers.

When Monday came around, sure enough, I began training the assistant superintendent's cousin on the art of data entry and information systems. She didn't have the skillset or work experience to perform the job, but I had to make this work. It took me more time and effort to have her do the job incorrectly, then redo the job correctly, all while having to watch out for every word that I said, knowing that it would all get reported back to my boss. I would have been better off not getting anybody at all.

—AMANDA MAMANI,
DATA AND ASSESSMENT COORDINATOR, HAWAII

Nepotism is not illegal, but it certainly can be damaging to an organization. The hiring of friends and family members who are not qualified to do the job creates resentment and animosity within the organization and slows down efficiency. We followed up with Amanda a few months later to find out that not only did the cousin get the job temporarily, but she didn't even have to go through the hiring process to put her on full-time status because she was already on the payroll. The assistant superintendent bypassed the hiring system to give his unqualified cousin the job—without an interview. The school board would never know, and nobody could ever say a word.

Amanda experienced the negative side of nepotism. While this situation does not pose a direct dunk tank situation for Amanda, her supervisor placed strategic chess pieces on the board for insulating himself against any of his own adversaries. Later on, Amanda was blamed for a few incomplete reports that were the responsibility of the new, unqualified cousin of the assistant superintendent. As accountability measures kicked in, Amanda was outnumbered by a family unit. Even though the terrible job performance was not due to Amanda's work quality, she eventually ended up in the dunk tank.

ADVERSARIAL TACTIC NO. 10: DEFLECTION

Blame is just a lazy person's way of making sense of chaos.
—DOUGLAS COUPLAND

My supervisor was rarely in the office; the earliest he would show up was 9:30 a.m. on a good day. Oftentimes, he would work from home or take a vacation day. Recently, he was promoted from curriculum director to deputy chief of academics. This meant more responsibility, different accountability measures, and more people to manage. For the past ten years as curriculum director, he was able to coast in the position on autopilot. Everyone who had worked with him during that time had learned to accept his inaccessible leadership style.

When I was hired as the ELA Coach, I was definitely the newbie in the department, and it was clear that they were a tight-knit group. As the weeks went on, the dynamics shifted and his employees began confiding in me. What I learned from them was that they were just playing the game. They knew the department wasn't efficient, they were frustrated that he never came to work, and they knew that he favored and protected Jake, in particular, but they also knew to just go along with it. Everyone wanted to fly under the radar and keep their jobs. When my supervisor did show up to the office, everything appeared fantastic, my colleagues kept everything surface level, and they didn't ask any questions or bring up anything significant. They knew just to keep things light and ignore all the real problems of the department.

As a newcomer to the department, one of my tasks was to take over managing the inventory. It had been Jake's job all along. I wanted to get this right because several principals had been calling me asking me for total counts on books, and they were frustrated that I didn't have the answers. What I soon discovered was that there was missing inventory, mixed up inventory, and uncatalogued inventory; it was clearly a mess. I asked Jake to share his inventory system with me, but to no avail. He didn't really have a system in place; he had some things on a spreadsheet, some things in the library database, and some things were just handed out and he didn't really know what the district had ordered.

During my next one-on-one meeting with my supervisor, I shared with her how the lack of systems and protocols was a barrier to our success; the need to get it all straight, even if we had to start over, was evident. This highly offended both Jake and my supervisor. Jake was so upset that he had to go home that day "sick." My supervisor was so upset that Jake was upset that he called me back into his office. He began by telling me that he had never lost an employee in his department, that it had always run smoothly, and that he didn't have any problems in the department until I showed up. He told me to figure out the inventory on my own and not to interact with Jake any longer. I was mortified. Obviously, they weren't looking for optimization, organization, or efficiency, and definitely not collaboration or input. They wanted somebody to play along with the dysfunction and pretend like Jake was doing a great job with the inventory.

—SHIAN WAKELY,
ELA COACH, SOUTH CAROLINA

The strategy of deflection is the art of turning the blame away from the root cause. In Shian's case, she was already up against other adversarial tactics. She was stepping into a department of nepotism, and her supervisor would protect Jake at any cost. What Shian didn't know at the time was that her supervisor had a close personal relationship with Jake outside of work. Several others in the department partied with this supervisor and also were in a tangled web of nepotism.

To make matters worse, Shian's supervisor was protected by the superintendent and the executive team, who would, in fact, extend professional courtesy as needed. Her supervisor was deflecting his own responsibility as a leader to show up at work and be accessible to her team. He was also deflecting his inappropriate relationship with Jake. It wasn't Shian's fault that the inventory was not correct or up to date; yet Shian would be the first one to take the fall for it. Shian was the newbie in town trying to assimilate to a new department, learning a new job, as well as trying to navigate the unspoken social rules and norms.

Shian was given the job of managing the book inventory of the district. Her intent was to get it organized, put systems into place, and have it accessible so that she could provide the principals with the proper information that they had requested. What she didn't realize was that she stepped on a landmine by discovering such a high level of dysfunction that it required deflection from every school leader who outranked her. Her supervisor quickly turned the blame and placed it on Shian, rather than on Jake, for not keeping copacetic records.

School leaders are told to "be strong," "build trust," "suck it up," "take the high road," or "make your adversaries your allies." But sometimes, that just doesn't work. Being aware of these ten adversarial tactics will assist you with "proactive paranoia," preparation, anticipation, and another important concept that we will discuss in the next chapter: the law of "aligned relatedness."

I cannot give you the formula for success, but I can give you the formula for failure, which is: Try to please everybody.

—**HERBERT SWOPE**

CHAPTER 4

UNDERSTANDING THE LAW OF ALIGNED RELATEDNESS

I heard the same requests every summer from the families in my neighborhood and at my church. They all wanted me to pull a favor and somehow magically enroll their child in my class. For whatever reason, my reputation in the community was that of a superhero or mythological god. I just did my teacher thing and inspired kids.

I taught like a pirate. I encouraged. I respected. I cared. That's it. What I would call the norm. It's what kids deserved. Making a difference seemed normal because it made me happy and it mattered. I went home every night feeling needed and successful.

—ROBERT GRAYSON,
SUPERINTENDENT, VERMONT

Robert's reputation of fervor and excellence had made its way through the community like a raging brushfire. Parents competed to make sure their child had the best teacher. They believed that Robert was the magic bullet to their child's future. In Robert's case, this worked for him. The chatter and curbside discussions were all very positive. Unfortunately, what we call "aligned relatedness" can work for you, but it can also equally work against you.

Magnetism, or the commonality of problems (having a problem in common), is where the law of "aligned relatedness" originates. Consider this story from Robert Grayson, who is no longer in the classroom but is now a superintendent of schools in Vermont:

I had no idea that everyone was connected in this town. Or, more accurately, the ones who were whackos found more whackos, who then had whacko friends and whacko relatives who came out of the woodwork . . . and I had no clue who these people were or where they came from. It was like the movie Invasion of the Body Snatchers *or some sort of zombie uprising.*

Every time I looked over my shoulder, a new accomplice was getting ready to set me up. It was exhausting. Talk about paranoia. My nerves were shot! And to think that this was a school district where we were supposed to be teaching kids and learning about teaching? Wow! Who would've thought that the politics in education were this lethal? It was crazy. Just crazy! You upset one person . . . just one person . . . and your career can end just like that!

Robert went on to tell us more about his attempt to help at-risk students in his small rural school district. He hired additional staff and reading-recovery personnel and unknowingly entered into a symbiotic, negative, aligned relatedness that worked against his career:

I put together a plan for our board of education and coordinated everything with our two elementary school principals regarding how to help our struggling readers. Everyone was on board, except one school board member whose child was actually going to receive reading recovery services. He was identified in the first week of first grade to need such services. We had tracked him throughout his kindergarten year and put various interventions into place that had not helped this board member's son.

We made presentations to the community and passed a budget, which included two reading-recovery teachers. We found these two teachers through a consortium of reading-recovery professionals, and they were incredible teachers. I even watched them teach during one of the interview segments where candidates had to provide direct reading-recovery instruction. It was beautiful. Just beautiful. These two teachers were the best of the best. So the teachers began their first year of reading recovery and about midway through December, I started getting phone calls from a few parents. Mind you: these were not reading-recovery parents, but strong community parents who had an issue with how many students were receiving reading recovery—which we all know is a low number due to the type of targeted intervention. Now, during our presentations and all throughout the entire process, everyone knew that reading-recovery teachers would have a very small student group. The goal was to keep the teacher-to-student ratio low. But this community member was upset that her tax dollars were being used only for a small number of students. She even accused me of looting the district and catering to my board member's kid.

It took me a while for this all to sink in, but at the January board meeting, there were fifty public comments about how I fooled everyone and hired my own friends to get a cushy teaching job with only a handful of students that they would have to service. I couldn't even identify some of these people in the crowd during public comments. Some of them were simply invisible to me. A coup was taking place, and I'm still not sure where the sneak attack originated. It was pure guerrilla warfare.

Then I looked over at my board and, low and behold, my board president was smiling while I was getting blasted during public comments. Was there a link? She wanted me gone as superintendent, but she got back on the board for another three-year term. I thought things were quiet, but I guess I was wrong. An army was forming against me. An army that snuck up on me. I stayed calm . . . I stood my ground . . . but it stunk for sure. I was getting blasted left and right and couldn't even identify where the shrapnel was coming from.

Robert's "proactive paranoia" was supercharged, but even while implementing this skill, he still could not clearly see his adversaries. They were in the trees throwing dunk tank balls downward—a sort of guerilla warfare, as Robert metaphorically characterized this situation.

While providing remedial, or RTI, services at the highest tier of intervention was approved by voters and by the board (so Robert thought), those who may have had a problem with the philosophy of reading recovery, staffing decisions, or even just Robert as the superintendent, rallied through the common magnetism of reading recovery as their shield to attack.

What started out as a philosophical disagreement about programming at Robert's school district turned into a tax-dollar bandwagon that would get others to support going against reading recovery and Robert. His adversaries had never met the Robert who had a waiting list of students who wanted to get into his classroom. They didn't know the heart Robert had for kids or his deep desire to make a positive difference. They didn't even care.

It may seem silly that adversarial conditions increased because of a literacy decision that was made and approved by the district, but this is Robert's reality. Aligned relatedness was at play here. The "magnetism of the cause" helped recruit other supporters to come out against Robert. As a result, he couldn't even discern the difference between his supporters and adversaries. His lens became blurred. The bottom line was people banded together to make Robert squirm.

Problems didn't stop there for Robert. Over a series of four more monthly board meetings (February–May), complaints about reading recovery turned into allegations of financial mismanagement. One board member even made a motion to have an external audit conducted by the State of Vermont Department of Education. Robert resided in a district of a new board majority of kamikazes who were willing to blow up

Robert's career, even if it meant not being re-elected for another board term.

Robert's school district became a headline within the community insomuch that his contract was not going to be renewed due to poor results for "fiscal planning and management" on his last year's evaluation. Today, Robert is still looking for work as a school superintendent. He shared with us how hard things were during the last year of his contract:

> *I was no longer allowed to hire any new staff. The board changed the hiring process so that I would not have a final interview process in order to determine which candidates would be recommended for hire. The board neutered me. I was a puppet during my final months on the job. And why? Because I brought reading recovery to the district? Because I wanted to help kids? I was a good leader, and I did good things for kids.*
>
> *It was so sad that I had to recommend new hires to the board, and I never met any of them in June of last year. The four principals held interviews and hired their staff. All I did was sign their contracts. I just can't believe how all of those people came out of the woodwork and turned everything into a "money mismanagement" issue. Now, I'm still without a job and can't pay my bills.*

LIKE ATTRACTS LIKE

It is the universal law of attraction. Have you ever noticed that groups of people can attract similar people—through the way they dress, their socio-economic status, their interests, their values, and their perceptions? More adversaries can be recruited by your current adversaries. They have friends who owe them a favor, perhaps. Or they like to see drama unfold.

In Robert's case, his "whackos attracted more whackos." It is no different in your workplace. The gossipers attract the gossipers, the innovators attract the innovators, and the lazy people attract more lazy people. Your adversaries gain power and justify their behavior by growing their numbers. If you upset one of them, you upset all of them. If you irritate one of the gossipers, you have irritated all of the gossipers (and they tell all their friends, too). If you support and lead the innovators, then you support and lead all of the innovators. It can work for you or against you depending on the awareness and intentionality of what you do as a school leader. Either way, the law of attraction is present, both positively and negatively.

When you begin a new job, you have to learn the policies and procedures of your new workplace and, at the same time, you should be watching the social dynamics to identify the subgroups of magnetism, likeness, or "aligned relatedness." Every organization has them. They are the unspoken social expectations based on the groups of like people who control the dynamic of the environment as a whole. Your new coworkers won't know the classroom version of you, the caring teacher within you, or your passion for making a difference. They will only see a new leader stepping onto their turf.

When moving up the food chain to district office, we wished we had been equipped with social leadership tools and enough *with-it-ness* to see things start to crumble around us. Even with an inkling of that knowledge, we would have handled ourselves differently. We're sure Robert would have done things differently, too, had he known what was about to happen. If we knew early in our leadership careers what we know now, we could have navigated the new rise in our careers more intentionally while preserving our own happiness and moral compass.

Every tier of leadership comes with a new set of social rules and expectations. A classroom teacher has to follow the social rules of the grade-level team. They align themselves with their like-minded people and follow the social expectations of the school, whether it is giving in to the social pressure to attend pot-luck luncheons, celebrate birthdays, or to hang out after school.

As a building administrator, a new set of social expectations is established among peers and with the district office. Administrators form alliances based on the law of attraction or aligned relatedness in order to survive. They must also follow the social lead of their district executive team, which may involve e-mailing late at night, meeting for social and community events, keeping the media at bay, and so on. You quickly learn what you can and can't do in order to stay under the radar and not upset the boss or people who no longer want you to be around. Unfortunately, "staying under the radar" can reduce your leadership power because, instead of automatically doing what's right, you filter every decision through the screen of "what might this decision do to me" paranoia.

New, unspoken social expectations, nuances, and social dynamics get more complicated the higher you climb within the hierarchy of education. You may have to deal with more red tape on any given issue. Robert, as superintendent, encountered an "invasion of the body snatchers" because of the unspoken social expectations and alliances that one adversary turned into dozens and dozens of vocal adversaries. The adversarial action of converting followers became too much for Robert to handle. There is power in numbers, even if those who are counted in the numbers are irrational, blind followers to people with hidden motives.

FAILING TO MEET EXPECTATIONS

Expectations can drive vengeful behavior. Consider the following story from a fifth-year, tenured middle school assistant principal who was attacked because she held to the policy of suspension for bullying. Her expectation was that her principal would back her decision. The assistant superintendent, whose stepson bullied another student, had an expectation that the assistant principal would look the other way. Both sets of expectations were in the line of crossfire.

> *I thought I was doing well. My principal loved me or, at least, used to love me. He recommended tenure for me two years ago. We had a good thing going. We had a solid school-wide behavior management plan, an anti-bullying program, tons of community resources for raising money for the kids, and about fifty academic and sports clubs set up for the kids. We were such a great team. My husband and I would meet him and his wife out for dinner every so often. We all got along really well—until I suspended a student for hazing another student in the locker room for the junior varsity football team that some of our eighth graders played on.*
>
> *I suspended the student for bullying another boy (he ripped his clothes and stole his pants and underwear in front of twenty students who were watching). The coach was still out on the field. Once I suspended the student, my principal backed down and didn't support me. I wondered why this was so, and even asked him. He told me to rescind the suspension and just shut up and not ask questions.*
>
> *I later learned that the student was a stepchild of the assistant superintendent. She believed the whole episode*

was dramatized—that it wasn't a major deal. In her eyes, I was the one who made it a major deal. Yet when I interviewed the other students as part of my investigation, it was a big deal.

As time passed, the whole thing got even messier. My secretary started getting phone calls about me. They would yell at her and tell her that they didn't want me talking to their child if they were sent down to me for any kind of discipline. The community started banding together against me. People I didn't even know, who never called my office, started joining the fight against me. They said my judgment was flawed. I lost all credibility. My principal told me I shouldn't have let things get this out of control . . . that I didn't listen to him and stuck to my guns even though it was his signature on the suspension letter.

I know I did the right thing, even though it meant that I ended up being moved to a new school. All of the negative attention I received was just brutal. My union got involved too, but this wasn't looked upon as a way for me to protect myself. It was perceived as me just starting more trouble. I had bit the hand that fed me. I questioned my supervisors. I disregarded everyone telling me to rescind my suspension recommendation. Now I don't even have the authority to suspend students on my own.

My principal signed it when it wasn't a big deal to anyone else other than the kid who was bullied. Neither of us knew who the perpetrator was; we thought this was a simple, straightforward discipline issue. No one knew the relationship between the student and the assistant superintendent or that the assistant superintendent would react this way in defense of her stepson. And all of the followers who supported the suspended student and the assistant superintendent came from everywhere, and my phone didn't stop ringing. There is support in numbers.

It is really scary. I still can't sleep over the whole thing. I was transferred to another middle school and everyone hates me there because they all know the bent story, not the real story. They see me as an enemy. I know I have to look for another job too. I hate going to work. I hate it.

—AMY HASKELL,
ASSISTANT PRINCIPAL, NEW HAMPSHIRE

There are so many layers to Amy's story. First, it is extremely difficult to know who is aligned with whom on every front and, in this case, the link between the suspended student and one of her supervisors was only one layer of not knowing where "aligned relatedness" existed. Second, although the principal could have rescinded the suspension, he didn't. Knowing that the train was already out of the station, he allowed it to appear as though Amy was the problem. The more firmly she stood her ground, the more believable it became that she, not the principal, had signed off on the suspension. As a result, her principal (who wanted to save his own neck) became her adversary.

What began as a student suspension quickly morphed into a hard lesson for Amy. Her credibility was now in question. Her stress level was high. She had been involuntarily transferred to a school with a principal who didn't want her there and colleagues assumed she was a poor decision-maker. Her peers and leaders at the new school had the dunk tank ready and waiting for her because they didn't have the facts—they just assumed she was guilty of wrongdoing.

Now let's shift to Nate O'Grady. Pay attention to how staying on top of potential "aligned relatedness" realities enabled him to navigate his way through his own superintendency within a highly political school district in Pennsylvania:

Do you know who Dean Weaver is? He is Josh Owens' youngest son who ran for town treasurer and lost. But now his uncle is running for the Republican Party nomination across town. He is the cousin of my board president and his girlfriend is a teacher at Oakley High School, so she has the inside scoop on anything that happens there. If you can't make Tricia happy, then you better get out of Dodge. Do you know who Katie Simmons is? She is Russ' ex-wife and Dean's daughter who is now running for the board in order to go after my middle school principal. If we can get our own insider to run against her, then we should be OK for at least three years; we would have control of the majority of the board for a little while.

Here, Nate knows the entire "family tree" of his district and state-wide division. He is "with-it" when it comes to relationships, friends, relatives, and connections across the community, and he understands how each one is tied to another by both visible and invisible strings. To further limit his dunk tank risks, Nate strategizes on getting folks to run for the board in order to make sure that the majority of those in power would be on good terms with him.

Unfortunately, education and politics go hand-in-hand. That truth means it is in the best interest of school leaders to know the intricacies of party politics, how an individual's or community's politics may impact school board candidacy, and how the political affiliations of those on the board will affect the way it governs. The reality is that politically driven candidates may or may not have good motives for wanting to acquire a board seat. Sadly, Nate's career strategy is a common one for superintendents who have to worry about board majorities, survival, and insulation. When leaders have to devote time and energy to strategizing how to save their necks, they have to less time and energy for the more important order of business: making decisions for kids.

Nate characterizes his board of education elections in a way that, while it may seem unfair, is so true. Notice how he labels his community supporters and adversaries:

> *In my eyes, there are only three types of board members: 1) those who want power to springboard their political careers, 2) those who have an axe to grind, or 3) those who truly have too much time on their hands. OK , maybe there is a fourth : those who truly want to help kids. But—c'mon, I've been to five different districts in the last twenty years of my career. I can't believe I've done this and survived for this long. The first three types really can beat the hell out of you. And while some might say that they are doing things for the kids, they have a second face that is looking at something totally different. Am I being unfair and pigheaded? Maybe. But what if I'm right and school leaders don't prepare themselves for a flurry of chaos that could take place if we are caught off guard? You have to remember—this is politics, like anything else.*

> *—NATE O'GRADY,*
> *SUPERINTENDENT, PENNSYLVANIA*

Nate recognizes that he could sound jaded, but he also states that "he has been around for a long time" and knows "how the game is played." He is a master at knowing the family trees of his communities, the family members, the friends, and the allies within those branches.

Aligned relatedness has the ability to impose indirect power and to impact an entire community (for good or bad). Aligned relatedness can also be as simple as a connected group of people who have a like-minded interest that are neither positive nor negative. We actually focus on three types of aligned relatedness: positive, negative, and neutral.

POSITIVE ALIGNED RELATEDNESS

A group of like-minded people who come together for a central commonality, interest, hobby, friendship, or belief can produce something beneficial to the greater community or people within the community. Notice some of the examples of positive aligned relatedness provided by some of our most interesting school leader participants in this book:

1. Nate O'Grady networked throughout the community and had a strong understanding of the connectedness of relationships. He used both his network and his insights to his advantage to arm the school board with strong members who would make genuine and sound decisions for the good of students and the district. The common focus helped minimize the risk of underlying agendas tainting the school board's decisions.

2. A group of school leaders who play bunko together on Friday nights got to talking about ways that they could help their community. The bunko group decided to sponsor a toy drive for the upcoming holiday.

3. Two of the administrative secretaries at a district's enrollment center noticed that the students who were in foster homes or group homes and were registering new to the district were often scared and felt like outcasts. These secretaries reached out to their friends at the other schools (whom they knew from church) to see if they

could make backpacks filled with school supplies, toiletries, clean socks, and a stuffed animal to make them feel special. They would also contact the principal of each school to see if it would be possible to assign a greeter to give each new foster or group home child a school tour and immediately assign them an adult with whom the child could check in each day for emotional support. Their efforts helped to meet the needs of these students whose home lives were complicated and unsettled.

4. A group of teachers who attended Zumba together after work every Tuesday and Thursday wanted to start a Fitbit challenge. They wanted to become more aware of their daily habits and focus on balancing the stress in their lives. They started a healthy competition to determine who had the most number of steps in a four-week period. They opened up the challenge to everyone on campus who wanted to join. Several teachers had been feeling stressed out and had put on a little weight. The competition was just what they needed! The competition ultimately turned into a fundraiser to benefit a few students who were having major surgeries.

5. A community member who volunteered at a Michigan school went to a luncheon benefitting a local foundation of which her brother was a co-chair. At the luncheon, her brother excitedly talked about the foundation's work and shared the news that it would be selecting the winner of the foundation's A+ School of Excellence award. After talking at length with her brother about the criteria, she believed the school for which she volunteered was an excellent candidate for the award. She called the

principal and encouraged him to apply for the award. Because the principal trusted this volunteer, who was also the vice-chairman of the city council, he submitted the application. The following year, his school was awarded A+ School of Excellence.

6. Several principals within a North Carolina school district who got along particularly well had started a book study together and were reading the book, *Multipliers*. In administrator meetings, they referred to principles in the book and used common language like: empire builders, leveraging talent, becoming a genius watcher, and so on. Their insights sparked conversation amongst administrators district-wide, and soon the book study expanded to include other district personnel. Because of the study, leaders throughout the district began building their academic empires as multipliers. They look for talent in others and intentionally created *new* multipliers. The study had a profound and positive effect on the culture of every school within the district.

NEGATIVE ALIGNED RELATEDNESS

A group of like-minded people who come together for a central commonality, interest, hobby, friendship, or belief can also produce something detrimental to the community or members within that community. Below are a few examples of negative aligned relatedness:

1. The narrative at the beginning of this chapter involving Superintendent Robert Grayson began as an innocent and productive support which ended in mutiny. He wanted to support struggling students with additional,

tiered instruction through a reading-recovery program. Rumors were generated and spread throughout the "anti-reading-intervention" community, and vocal members claimed the reading initiative was rigged and mismanaged. His adversaries misconstrued facts and told lies that generated a negative aligned relatedness against Robert. When the adversarial tactic of rumors kicked into full gear, Robert's career did not stand a chance. Someone had to take the fall for this community escapade, and it sure wasn't going to be the school board.

2. Amy Haskell experienced negative aligned relatedness when her principal expected her to extend professional courtesy for suspending a student for bullying. She was expected to look the other way because the student was the stepchild of the assistant superintendent. Instead, she adhered to her moral compass and stood by her ethical decision. Unfortunately, the adversarial tactic of deflection was launched, and her career and reputation suffered to the point that she is now looking elsewhere for work.

3. Several people from a district office in Washington, including the superintendent, assistant superintendent, and two principals get together on the weekends to golf. On the golf course, their conversations often turn to work-related conversations and, more specifically, criticisms of other people in their district. One of the principals asked if they had heard about the new district transportation director. This principal said he had heard that the director was already calling in sick to work and telling the employees he had a terminal illness. The

assistant superintendent chimed in and said that several of the bus drivers had complained that the transportation director overreacted to things and watched their timecards like a hawk. In the weeks that followed this conversation, the superintendent talked with a couple more bus drivers who complained that the director was not really getting along with the new employees. The two principals buddied up to the new director to try to befriend him and get a little more information out of him. He told them about an undiagnosed health issue he was having and about the different medications he was trying. During the leaders' next golf game, the conversation once again focused on the transportation director. Together, they decided they wanted him gone. The bus drivers, two of whom were longtime friends of the superintendent, didn't like the director. They worked out a plan: The superintendent would speak with the human resources department and recommend that the director be put on disability. Rather than going through the protocol and chain of command to address a possible problem, these golfing buddies were more interested in using the adversarial tactics of nepotism and using (and bending) the power of information.

NEUTRAL ALIGNED RELATEDNESS

A group of like-minded people who come together for a central commonality, interest, hobby, friendship, or belief may meet without causing any specific positive or negative outcome. That said, this neutral relatedness often opens the door to future connections and outcomes. Take a look at these examples of neutral aligned relatedness:

1. A group of several teachers, an instructional coach, and the president of the local educational foundation all love the outdoors. They coordinate and organize a time to go on a hike to enjoy the outdoors and one another's company. Nothing results from their gathering, except for creating the opportunity for all kinds of "relatedness" to be built.

2. An assistant director of student services has a son who is big into horse roping and made the national team as a result of his skills. Whenever her son is in town for a competition, several employees join her at the roping competition and cheer on her son. Nothing results from their night out, except for a friendly exchange and an opportunity to deepen friendships.

3. In a small town with a big religious presence, many of the employees of a school district attend the same denominational church. There is a big revival in town and many of these employees attend the religious event over the weekend and become even more supportive and encouraging to one another even at school, but because of the large number of participants, nothing results from their revival event other than the recognition of their own identities as Christians and the potential for friendships to be built.

Neutral aligned relatedness is a concept that is different from positive or negative aligned relatedness in that it simply establishes the *potential* for positive or negative results. The connection itself is a neutral event or incident, even if it is communal in nature. In other words, neutral aligned relatedness can become positive or negative aligned relatedness depending on what each group decides to do with the gathering. If a group's members have adversarial goals, then an army of adversaries will be gathered, similar to Robert Grayson's situation. If a neutral event is to attend a weight loss walk, then the outcome of a fundraiser being created from that neutral event becomes a positive aligned relatedness.

In all three types of aligned relatedness, we see that like attracts like. Nothing is innately wrong with like-minded groups of people coming together. After all, we are social beings. Gathering or uniting with people who share our interests feels natural and comfortable. It has happened since the beginning of time and will continue to happen in every community, neighborhood, and organization. Aligned relatedness worked for Robert Grayson as a classroom teacher. But as you saw from his story, it worked against him as a superintendent. The caution regarding aligned relatedness comes when a group becomes self-serving, corrupt, or toxic. One idea or wrong connection, no matter how small, can spiral out of control. The moral of this story is to be aware of the connections, relationships, and politics within your organization and community so you can align with groups that will support rather than attack you.

To have long-term success as a coach or in any position of leadership, you have to be obsessed in some way, but not possessed.

—**PAT RILEY**

CHAPTER 5

RECONSIDERING FIFTEEN-HOUR WORK DAYS

There weren't enough hours in a day to plan lessons for all my kiddos, let alone keep up with my caseload of forty-three IEP's. This meant forty-three meetings before or after school or during my prep or lunch. But I did it. I knew it was right, and forty-three was not a number, they were my kids. They deserved individual instruction, strategies, and success.

I'm not going to lie, I had to drink a lot of coffee, my family suffered, and time with my friends was non-existent. I had to stay up until midnight to finish one IEP for a 7:00 a.m. appointment the following day. I was lucky if I managed to show up to the meeting with matching shoes and my hair combed. But I did it, because, to that child, it mattered. To those parents, it mattered. And then I had to do it forty-two more times. Like Dory, I had to "just keep swimming, just keep swimming." I mean, who else is going to advocate for these kids if I don't?

—Craig Duffy,
Director of Special Education, Mississippi

Overworked and underpaid is the name of the game in education, but the expectation set for Craig was a formula for crashing and burning. He burned the midnight oil and maintained the pace, but maybe he should have reconsidered when and how to do business.

THE HEALTH RISKS OF OVERWORKING

There are two ways to live life as a school leader: 1.) You can live a balanced life where being a school leader comes *after* your personal and family priorities; or 2.) You can live a life where your career drives you to do everything you can (for as many hours each day as you can stand) in order to prevail.

Sometimes, our biggest problems might not be our adversaries, but the bills we have to pay, the families we have to support, or the expenses that rear their heads when we have a toothache or prescription to purchase. It is easy to say, "You have to be balanced," or "Work is not the most important thing in life; family is," or "This isn't worth it." But we remember what it is like to slog through long days—week after week—while trying to figure out ways to prevail in circumstances that were detrimental to our health and sanity. In extreme situations, the tendency is to "just do it," but that is a short-term, unsustainable solution.

There are some school leaders who don't seem to have a care in the world. They don't get stressed because their day is shorter than that of most of the students in their schools. They swing by the office after 9:00 a.m. and are out before the students are on their buses ready to head home. Meetings don't phase them; they don't bring a pad of paper with them or even bother to take notes on a napkin for that matter. These carefree individuals simply coast through their careers, collecting huge paychecks along the way.

Then there are the school leaders who take things too seriously. Perfectionists. Control freaks. Dare we say "anal-retentive beings"? These are the school leaders who answer and send e-mail at all hours. They arrive early, the sleep still clinging to their eye lashes. They flip on the lights and rationalize that they will be able to "get so much work done while the office is quiet." They stay late, even though they haven't seen their children for a few nights in a row because of board meetings and school functions.

We have been those perfectionist leaders. And we *now* know that no one will ever remember if we came in early or were the last ones to leave at night. Quite honestly, no one cares—except the overachievers inside of us. And while we spent so much time at work trying to defeat or appease our adversaries—effectively making them our No. 1 priority—life passed us by. The question we should have asked much earlier in our careers is this: *Should our adversaries even be our number one task?*

Many authors and thought leaders encourage us to ignore the negative, focus on the positive—ignore the garbage and focus on building greatness. We don't disagree with this message; we just contend that, when it comes to adversarial conditions, ignoring the perpetrators or their actions is not an option.

Adversaries will do anything in their power to make your life miserable. There will never be enough hours in a day to combat their toxicity because they will prepare, work, plot, pillage, or plunder harder and longer than you can possibly imagine. *You become *their* full-time job*—and they will work overtime to drown you.

Craig Duffy is now a special education director. Unfortunately, he got caught up in a major lawsuit regarding a potential violation of a child's IEP (which was never actually violated). Here's how the stress affected him:

> *I just became so run down. I seemed to always have a terrible cold and a lack of energy. I worked and worked and worked to counteract everything that they [my adversaries] were doing to me. I sought new personal references for myself, even looked for a new position just to get out of here, but it was like a plastic bag being placed over my face trying to kill me. My nemesis spent all of his time coming after me, so much that it felt like it was his full-time job. I couldn't stay afloat any longer. I just crumbled. Arriving to the office at 5:00 a.m. and not leaving until well after 8:00 p.m. on a good night was just a recipe for disaster. I hardly ate. My stomach was always in knots. I was an absent husband and father. This was no way to live. It wasn't worth it. No way.*
>
> —CRAIG DUFFY,
> DIRECTOR OF SPECIAL EDUCATION, MISSISSIPPI

Craig's story is no different from anyone who, under the pressure of adversarial conditions, thought that working harder, longer, or smarter was the answer. In Craig's case, he was facing litigious parents who sued the district *annually* because the district-level special education decisions for their children did not match their desires. Craig strove to do what was right and to do his best, but even that didn't keep him out of the dunk tank.

THE SEARCH FOR PERFECTION

Sometimes we are our own worst enemies when we are working to fix our adversarial conditions. Consider the following story of Janine, a principal who feels as if she has no choice but to be "perfect":

> *If I make one mistake, my superintendent is going to go nuts. I am under the gun and know that he doesn't want me here. During a layoff due to a few schools closing, I was able to keep my job because I have more seniority than two other secondary principals. So they had to find new jobs and I'm still here—but barely living and surviving. I know my superintendent liked the other principals more than me. They were part of the old boys' club and I'm, well . . . first, I'm not a boy, and I'm not old either! You know what I mean. They were all tight. I was the outsider. Now I'm the only one standing, and my superintendent believes the only reason I'm still here is because I'm female. I know he wants me out so he can bring back one of his buddies.*
>
> *Ever since the layoff, he has made my life a living hell. Up means down and down means up. White means black and red means fury for him. I remember just sending an e-mail to a parent yesterday, and I had bcc'd my superintendent so he was aware of a discipline issue. He called me after opening the e-mail and started screaming at me for misspelling the parent's name. (And he says I'm the*

*one who is "too emotional.") That's just a spelling mis-
take on one e-mail. It isn't the end of the world; but right
now, I have to be perfect. I'm trying to convince my body
that I don't need much sleep anymore. Even if I have to
work day and night to make sure that no mistakes exist
on anything, I have to do it. Nothing. No mistakes. Zilch.
I have to be perfect. I really can't mess up. Or else.*

—JANINE VELEZQUEZ,
HIGH SCHOOL PRINCIPAL, MASSACHUSETTS

Janine realizes that her job, while not affected by a recent
batch of layoffs, remains in jeopardy. Her struggle to be perfect
consumes her attitude, mind, spirit, and daily task list. What she
cannot accomplish during the day, she tackles at night. Janine
informed us that she works most of the day and night and only
takes intermittent breaks to eat, go to the gym, or attend church
on Sunday. She doesn't have a personal life. This job is all that
she has. She is single, lonely, and sad about where she is working.
She tried looking for a new position in another school district a
few months ago, but she never received a call for an interview.
As a result, Janine's own *unhealthy* paranoia is getting the best
of her:

*I find it hard to believe that after four or five applications
. . . not one call for an interview. Not one. Am I being
blackballed? Is my superintendent not giving me a good
reference because he hates me? I would almost think that
he would want to give me a good reference so I could leave
and then be out of his hair. That way, he could reinstate
one of his buddies.*

*I just don't get it. It should be the reverse here. Give me
a great reference and be done with me. I'm a great principal. The staff and students are wonderful. We get along*

great. I try to reflect on everything that I've done and everything that I do. I try to assess if it's me who is the problem. I'm starting to think it is. I'm not myself. I'm a train wreck.

Janine's own dunk tank experience has taken such a toll on her that she is questioning her abilities and self-worth. That's the power of being in the dunk tank; we wonder what we've done wrong. We assume the position of victim, and at the same time believe ourselves to be at fault. Working harder and harder is our recourse for trying to make things right—because our effort is the only thing over which we have any control. We want to do things the right way and succeed. After all, no one *wants* to fail.

The long hours are only crippling Janine's ability to think straight, to make decisions cohesively, and to be an effective leader. The search for perfection will only end up killing Janine's career—and damaging her health. She believes that her work ethic is all that she has control over, but it is this type of control that will eat her alive.

SEEKING REVENGE

A natural response when we feel beaten down is to push back, fight, and try to defeat our adversaries. The problem with this reaction and the driving emotion of vengefulness is that it will test our faith, ethics, and morals, and leave us feeling empty even if we succeed in our efforts to beat our adversaries. Revenge is an identity-altering form of human agency that leads to disharmony, confusion, and negative mindsets. In the following narrative, Jessie Malber shares the struggle he feels with his decision to work against his principal:

Ron [the principal] is a jerk. He deserves what he gets. He comes in late and leaves early. I end up doing all the work. The staff hates him. They like me. The parents hate him. They like me. I'm there 24/7. He swoops in for a couple of hours, makes all the wrong decisions, and I am left with cleaning up his messes. The teachers' union building reps look to me for answers. They talk trash about Ron. I don't actively try to set Ron up, but I guess I don't really protect or defend him, either. So the union sees how I'm being passive, and they take that as their answer. Everyone wants me to be the principal. I hear the parents talking about Ron, too. When I walk by, they don't try to hide it. They just say, "Oh, there's Jessie, the real principal," and I don't respond when I probably should. But I just get so angry about being the go-to guy for everything. Ron gets paid twenty thousand dollars more than me, and I do all of the work. It stinks. It's not right.

Here, Jessie's form of revenge is passive; he feels hostility toward Ron but is not actively insubordinate or overtly rude. The salary-to-workload discrepancy adds to his feelings of resentment. While Jessie spends all of his time working, he doesn't spend one moment supporting Ron. Jessie indirectly fuels Ron's own dunk tank and, up to this point, Ron has survived. Little does he know, however, he is headed down a path of a "vote of no confidence" from two out of three of his bargaining units, including the teachers' union. Jessie's silence is his own weapon of choice.

Like it or not, we must support our supervisors, even if we feel we are better workers, better problem solvers, better at public relations, or better at *anything* (you name it). Supporting leaders (and not sabotaging—even passively) when we don't agree with their tactics or work ethic is akin to taking the high road. Doing the right thing, for the good of the school or district, means fostering unity, not dissention, through our actions, words, and silence. If you are seen as divisive, you may be next in line for the dunk tank.

Jessie will have to live with his lack of action and learn how to support anyone and everyone even if doing so goes against what seems fair. It is our duty to not contribute to dunk tank situations because, in the end, we are only hurting ourselves and creating a weaker organization for children. Jessie's fifteen-hour days are apprentice related. He is an entry-level school leader who doesn't have to work long hours in order to survive. What gets done gets done and what doesn't get done won't. Here, fifteen-hour work days are spent on details and managing the entire ship for both the captain and co-captain's duties when he should be spending at least some of his time building a team, supporting his principal, and looking at this experience as an example of what not to do in the future. Fueling the fire against Ron will only end up hurting Jessie's true identity in the end.

THE MARTYR EFFECT

For some educators, like Janine Velezquez, the desire to be perfect is a response to dunk tank circumstances beyond their control. Others feel the need to outperform their peers. But some educators, like Sarah in the narrative below, work long days for more dysfunctional reasons:

> *I just happen to be a very efficient worker. It is in my DNA. I have always been able to multitask and accomplish at least double the work compared to my peers. When given a project, I invariably beat the deadline.*

Even back in grade school, I never took any work home or needed to complete homework because I always used my time efficiently while in class. This served me well later as a teacher because there were so many tasks and deadlines to manage and juggle—grading, calls, data entry, and preparations. This, too, I was able to master and, as a result, was able to consistently leave at a reasonable time every day. I have never believed in working for the sake of working. Harmony, balance, and sustainability have been my mantras.

When I moved to the district office, I expected a higher level of demand, and I was prepared to work extra hours and put in every effort necessary to succeed. What I discovered after about six weeks was that I had once again mastered the art of efficiency in my role. While I had mastered this art, it was clear that my peer, Sarah, the math coordinator in my department, had not. One late afternoon as I slid my purse on my wrist and reached for my keys to leave for the day, I heard her mumble, "I'm so glad that someone around here gets to go home at a reasonable hour. I've been at this all day and I've still got about three more hours ahead of me."

I offered to help, but to no avail; her work wasn't anything that I had been trained on nor did I have enough background knowledge to accomplish the task. On another occasion, I offered to assist with her late-night work and she accepted. However, not only did she accept my help, but she seemed to be vengeful by listing several unmanageable tasks for me to do. She ended the sentence with, "And I'll need all that by morning." As if this proved that the workload in our office was inequitable and she was burdened with so much more to do. Sarah was making the task so unmanageable that I couldn't complete it without staying up to all hours of the night myself. After watching this behavior pattern day after day, week after week, I noticed what was really happening. During the day, Sarah would flutter around from one department to the next visiting with coworkers, talking with principals and coaches on the phone, and socially networking. She would finally settle in sometime after lunch to start doing her work. There was always a justification for staying hours past everyone. "The superintendent needs this report tonight, and I'm leading the assistant principals' meeting tomorrow," or "The curriculum map is due to the principals right away." What I was seeing was time being squandered at work during the day. Habitually, Sarah had to be the last one to leave and she consistently sent late night e-mails just to prove that she worked the hardest. Although I am a team player and desired to fully carry my weight in the department, it seemed to be an infeasible task. She was feeding off of the attention and dramatizing her workload just to play the martyr. It wouldn't have mattered how late I stayed to help her; she would have stayed later anyway.

—Chloe Bushnell,
ELA Curriculum Specialist, Wyoming

Periodically, we run into educational martyrs like Sarah. While many leaders are genuinely overworked, overburdened, or perfectionists by nature, some simply have the need to be seen as carrying the biggest workload.

In this scenario, Chloe was a self-assured and efficient individual who lived a balanced lifestyle. And although Chloe takes pride in her work and is a team player, she doesn't have a need to stand out. Sarah, on the other hand, had an essential need to be viewed as the hardest worker in the department and, as a result, would mismanage her time so that she *appeared* irreplaceable.

She needed to be needed. Her efforts were a smoke-and-mirrors attempt to cement her own job security.

What Sarah didn't realize was that she was slowing down the organization and, in the end, she was using her personal time to do it. Did Sarah feel threatened by others? Quite possibly. Did she have a personal life outside of work? Possibly not. Did she have something to prove? Probably. Obviously, there was a deep, psychological reason for Sarah's martyrdom. Maybe she was jealous of Chloe.

Thankfully, once Chloe tuned in to Sarah's behavior patterns, she no longer felt guilty leaving at a decent hour, nor did she continue to offer to stay late into the evening to further enable Sarah's martyrdom. As a team player, it is easy to get pulled into staying later and later when those around you are burning the midnight oil. We can stand back and simply tell you to say "no" to the things that you cannot tack onto your to-do list, but this chapter goes deeper than that. Just because those around you are working late and sending e-mails at all hours of the night doesn't mean that you need to feel obligated to do the same. We are not just telling you to say "no" to projects that you should not take on when you have your own long laundry list of work to do. We are urging you to look at the driving forces behind long hours and lots of work. Here, martyrdom was at play. Once Chloe recognized the tactic, the dunk tank became inoperable. In your own career, be aware of peers or leaders who might be playing the martyr card and refuse to play their game.

THE HUNGER TO ADVANCE

Chances are you chose the field of education because you wanted to make a difference. In fact, most educators are in the business of serving the community and putting student achievement ahead of their own needs—even if that requires putting in long days on occasion. But there are those in education whose driving motive is getting ahead. They are willing to put in excessive hours in hopes of earning a better title. Let's examine a scenario about a federal programs director who allowed work to preoccupy every aspect of his life. Tune in and notice what his administrative secretary says about her boss's all-consuming motive to advance his career:

> *Nearly every day was the same broken record. I would receive a call from the Chief Academic Officer (CAO) and Rafael (my director) would run down to her office to meet at her beck and call. Rafael would return with a steno pad filled out front and back with another long list of things to do. He would agree to do anything for her, last minute, even if it wasn't anywhere near the jurisdiction of our department.*
>
> *It was my job to manage Rafael's calendar and fit in everything. I needed to set appointments on his calendar to follow up with principals, gather data on the instructional coaches, organize the luncheon for the district secretaries' meeting, redo the assessment graphs to look at the data in a different way, check in with the other departments to put in an office supply order, all while planning and coordinating the district-wide professional development day. Rafael was literally the CAO's puppet. He wanted to advance his career so badly that he was willing to take on work outside his department, do menial tasks, and work all hours of the night just to try to impress the CAO.*
>
> *Many times I overheard personal phone calls in Rafael's office that sounded like this: "Mom, I'm not going to be able to help you tonight. I've got this really big project*

I'm working on, and I have to do this if I want to ever move into an assistant superintendent position." Or "Hi, honey, I'm not going to make it home for dinner tonight, so just go ahead and feed the kids. Hopefully I will be back before you go to bed. I gotta do this, honey, if I am going to make it to the next level; I just have to put in my time. It is just the price we have to pay to get to the next level."

Rafael was leashed to his phone. He answered texts at all hours of the night and responded to e-mails within minutes. He always told me about how much he worked. I was afraid that he would eventually crash and burn. I could look at things objectively, but he couldn't see the storm that he was creating. He really didn't have a life other than work.

—*MARIETTA SCHMIDT,*
ADMINISTRATIVE SECRETARY, NEVADA

For some people, the need to advance their careers becomes all-consuming. They find themselves in sell-your-soul situations—trading their lives for (the hope of) a better title. Rafael had become a slave to advancement. Marietta was not only managing the department, she was managing Rafael's career. Rafael was fixated on demonstrating that he was a valued asset to the district, hoping that his non-stop efforts would lead to career advancement.

We did a follow-up interview with Marietta a few months after she shared this story with us. She told us then that the CAO understood Rafael's driving desire and purposefully took advantage of it. She found it easy to just pass off the projects because she knew he would accomplish the tasks. She had no intention of promoting Rafael, and had no problem using him as her minion. And why not? She knew he would do anything that she wanted. The CAO essentially preyed on Rafael's weakness—his thirst for advancement.

Rather than focusing on leadership presence, doing a quality job in his department, or managing his time well, Rafael focused on advancing his career. As educators, we must be careful not to let ambition slip into the category of self-gain or self-service. When we have a "willing to do anything to get to the next level" attitude, we may end up, like Rafael, as a puppet performing in a play with no end or reward.

Various motives push people to work fifteen-hour days. Many of us, like Craig Duffy, are dedicated to students and have to deal with inordinately high expectations. Some educators feel like work slaves because of pressures put on them by adversarial conditions. And still others create their own difficult circumstances. But one thing all midnight-oil-burners have in common is a deteriorated quality of life. While it may be possible to endure the work load for a time without losing your sanity or health, most of us cannot maintain the imbalance long term. The vicious cycle of long days can lead to malnutrition, the use of stimulants, or the need for medical intervention because of high anxiety, stress, or overexertion. No advancement or extreme level of dedication is worth compromising your health and well-being. You must be intentional enough to say, "No!"

It is absurd that a man should rule others, when he cannot rule himself.
—Latin Proverb

CHAPTER 6

Facing Alcohol, Pills, and Dependency

I had a dream job teaching sixth-grade math. The kids were at the perfect age where you could make a big impression on the rest of their lives. I loved math and I loved kids. One plus one equals two. Voilà! It was the perfect recipe for a lifetime of job satisfaction.

Mine was the classroom that the principal always dropped in on when someone "important" was on campus. Principal Stallward would stand at the back of the room, and I could see him pointing over to the posters the kids had generated with new strategies on how to solve *mathematical equations in new ways. They would gaze at my objectives that included technology integration and were aligned to my essential questions and standards. Then they would walk around the room, kneeling down to talk with kids about their learning. Every visit was ended with a high-five from Principal Stallward and a kind note left on my desk. I had quite a collection of them, and each and every one of those notes gave me more confidence and job satisfaction. I mattered. Why would I ever want to leave this profession? I have the greatest job on earth!*

—Darlene Murphy,
K–12 Math Curriculum Specialist, Indiana

This is a snapshot of who Darlene really is, deep down inside: a top-notch, engaging math teacher. Her kids always showed the most growth in math, and, more importantly, she would leave her students wanting to pursue a career that used math because they thought it was so much fun.

But here is where this chapter is going to make a U-turn and head to the deepest, darkest depths of education and the dunk tank. What you're about to read may seem hard to believe. And we're almost certain you've never before read anything about this topic in a book for educators. It's very unorthodox for academic publishers to allow the inclusion of such content, but our school leaders' stories *need* to be told.

Before we move forward and provide you with some very emotionally saddening stories, please know that the intent of this book is to help you with your present or future dunk tank struggles on any level, deep or shallow, grave or minor. We are not sharing these stories because they represent all school leaders. We are sharing them because, even though these school leaders may very well be in the minority, they can teach us an awful lot about who we are, where we have been, and where we need to go. Let's first look at what Darlene had to say about her life as a math curriculum specialist working in a district office:

I just couldn't take it anymore. I woke up one morning on a Saturday and my heart was racing. I was trembling. My hands couldn't even hold a glass of orange juice. All I could think about was work and how my supervisor wanted to fire me so he could bring in one of his close friends. I've been with the district for fifteen years, worked incredibly hard to become part of the team, but then, with no rhyme or reason, he just wanted me gone. I had a lot on my plate. I was balancing fifteen projects compared to the six or seven that my supervisor gave to his other curriculum specialists. Why was I getting overloaded? It was like he was trying to break me, and you know what? He did.

I told my husband that I had to go to the doctor right away, so he drove me there on a Saturday. Luckily, my primary doctor had walk-in hours on Saturdays from 10:00–12:00. When I got there, I walked in with fear and anxiety and came out with a prescription for Zoloft® and Xanax®. Anti-depression drugs. Anti-anxiety drugs. I felt like a failure because I needed medication just to stay even-keeled.

The Xanax worked right away. I could feel a calmness come over me whenever I felt anxious about my job. Not my life. Just my job, which sometimes felt like the only life I had. The Zoloft took weeks to regulate itself within my body. My problem was that I was drinking alcohol heavily too—more than I ever had. It started out as one or two glasses of wine with dinner, but it immediately turned into a 750 ml bottle each night. Throw in a Xanax, and whew! I felt great! My problems went away when I was hammered. But each day got worse.

I started drinking a 1.75 liter bottle of wine each night. My husband was a big drinker himself, so he didn't really think much about how much I was consuming. I just wanted to forget about my problems. Feel laid back. Push my problems under the rug.

After a while, I just self-destructed. It affected my work. I was always popping a pill and pouring a glass of wine the second I left the office. My office staff knew how much I loved to drink, and I think they condoned it, inadvertently. They bought me cute painted wine glasses with slogans written on them like, "Don't talk to me until I've had my WHINE," or "Coffee is for the morning, wine is for the rest of the day."

My Facebook postings always talked about having a bottle of wine or drinking in general when I look back on them now. I took pictures of cocktails that I would try making. Everything revolved around pills and booze.

Finally, my friends told me I needed help and, instead of fighting them, I realized they were right. I went on to resign from my job simply because of the stress.

—Darlene Murphy,
K-12 Math Curriculum Specialist, Indiana

Darlene shared her very personal experiences as part of this chapter—a chapter that demonstrates the power of how the dunk tank can lead us into our own self-defeating "drink tank." Her story illustrates how easy it is to lose control. When that happens, it's as if we're stepping up to the dunk tank platform even if we haven't been summoned.

THE DARK SIDE OF EDUCATION

Through our interviews with so many colleagues, this was the one topic that nobody wanted to admit, at first, but did share after understanding how we would use their stories and protect them with pseudonyms.

Ralph Klessing is one of those brave leaders who shared his experiences, and we cannot thank him enough for helping to expose the dark side of education. Here is part of his story:

I felt like I was secretly struggling alone until I found out my colleagues were all on Xanax, Ativan® or another variant of the benzodiazepine family. Literally. All of the coworkers in my department. They all managed their anxiety through prescription medication. Even though it felt liberating to know that I wasn't alone, it seemed abhorrent at the same time. What could be so awful that everyone required prescription medication to tolerate getting through a day at work in the field of education? This was the point at which I realized that the problem really wasn't me. If so many of my colleagues were affected in the same manner, it couldn't be just me causing my own tension in my district. My biggest struggle was sleeping. The insomnia, coupled with episodic anxiety attacks, was killing me.

I remember the piercing sound of my director's voice as she entered the office for the day: my heart would begin racing like a stampede of horses in the Kentucky Derby ready to leap right out of my chest. It took mindful breathing and conscientious calming strategies to get my anxiety under control so that it didn't turn into a full-blown panic attack. At one point, it was so bad that one of my colleagues excused herself for the day, saying that she didn't feel good and immediately went to the ER and checked

127

herself into the hospital where they ran an EKG and a whole barrage of tests that they conduct for typical heart issues. She was so young, so it seemed unlikely that she would have an issue. The conclusion was that Brinley's heart was strong but her struggle with anxiety was real.

A joke around the office was that it was a "Wambien" kind of day. Meaning that, in order to get to sleep, we would need to pop an Ambien and chase it with a glass of wine. We were even pill-sharing in the office. One of our colleagues, who was new to the office, was hit by the curse of anxiety for the first time. Like clockwork, everyone swung around in their office chairs to face her and, like a team of rehearsed synchronized swimmers, we all reached into our top drawers and pulled out our prescription bottles.

We all had our own stories. Brinley pushed her bottle forward toward Danielle and said, "Here, this will help; it's Klonopin. It suppresses the central nervous system, and will slow your heart rate and breathing right away, so you definitely need to get an appointment with your doctor to get some. It will take several visits for your doctor to prescribe something like this. We can help you out until you get your own prescription." And just like that, Danielle became one of us.

—RALPH KLESSING,
PROFESSIONAL DEVELOPMENT COORDINATOR

Pills were a survival tool in this stressful, hostile work environment. The adversarial conditions pushed in from all directions—their superintendent, a few principals, lots of board members—and the director led her staff to believe that they needed to work harder, be less collaborative, be more obedient, and compromise their moral compass in order to make it at the district office level. Abusing medication is sometimes the only way "out" for leaders who are stressed out or "under the gun." It is not the default defense mechanism, but pain is still a reality that happens in every state and maybe even in every district. We all handle things differently. We are human beings. The problem is that nobody has been willing to talk about it. Until now.

Some school leaders compromise their morals by trying to assimilate to the culture of the district office life. Some of them followed and led unspoken social rules that dominated their offices. After all, neither Brinley nor Danielle had ever worked at the district office level before, so they didn't have anything to compare it to. They justified that this was the price that they had to pay in order to work at this level. Toward the end of our interview with Brinley Winters, she shared the following insights:

> I lost a little bit of myself, piece by piece, along the way. Through this self-doubt, I found my heart racing every time one of "them" turned the corner. I was anxious driving to work and anxious driving home. I never slept and was always overtired. My coworkers were leaving during the work day to check in at the ER for blood pressure readings. It was clearly a hostile work environment. But for four years, I kept giving them the benefit of the doubt, thinking that it would get better. I wasn't a quitter. I wasn't a bad person. I told myself that I needed to get better at playing the game.
>
> I had positive intentions. I really did. After all, the good people who chose to be in the educational field were not in it for the money; they were invested in the community and in kids. Right? I was wrong about a few educators and finally reached my threshold and self-realization of where I was and who I had become. I didn't like myself. Everything was on the down-low, whispered, secret

texts, avoiding security cameras. I was operating in the underworld of a secret society with unspoken rules, all hidden from anyone outside looking in. It was all a disgrace to the taxpayers, illegal to auditors, and 100 percent compromising of the moral oath we promised when becoming certified. I wanted out, I needed out, and I had no immediate escape to another position. So I resigned and got help.

—BRINLEY WINTERS,
ELL SPECIALIST, OKLAHOMA

Brinley and her entire department of coworkers were all in a dunk tank prison. But how did they get there? They each started out highly competent for their positions and passionate about their work. They were good people who were hired to do good work. But it's like the analogy of the frog in a boiling pot of water. If you put a frog in a pot of boiling water, it will hop right out. But if you put the frog in a pot of lukewarm water and slowly turn up the heat, it will surely die.

Brinley, Danielle, and their entire department's experiences were no different. Each entered a lukewarm environment. The behavior patterns of their adversaries were not obvious because they were strategic enough, slow enough, covered up enough, passive aggressive enough to never let the newcomer know that they were trapped in a pot before the flame was turned up. Overt or subconscious, knowingly or unknowingly, dunk tanks were activated. Danielle, Brinley, and the entire crew in their department became trapped by corruption, trapped in fear, and trapped in literally physically damaging anxieties.

The dunk tank curse is real. If Brinley had seen the horrors of the department within the first week of work, it may have been evident to her that it was a hostile work environment and a place where morally wrong decisions were being made. But that didn't happen because things appeared collaborative, and her coworkers appeared satisfied to the naked eye. Little did Brinley know that her coworkers were all covering up a multitude of sins within the organization. Nor did they know that, to cope with the stress and fear of working in such conditions, their coworkers were dependent on anxiety medications.

We are not blaming Danielle or Brinley for not seeing the reality for what it was; we are simply using their experience as a warning about how complicated life can get for school leaders who face hostile or exceptionally stressful conditions. We are also *not* saying that, when things get tough, you too will become an alcoholic or addict.

Our goal is to support you and equip you with insights about real-life dangers. You might even be able to relate on some level to these stories. If so, we urge you to practice proactive paranoia and aligned relatedness strategies. Be mindful about the organization and others' intentions that may not be noble. You may even need to simply escape from your workplace for good—for *your* own good.

THE DOUBLE-EDGED SWORD OF ANTI-DEPRESSANTS

We are not opposed to prescription medication. We realize that some people really need it (and it often works wonders for large numbers of patients throughout the world). However, the flip side of this conversation is that our lives are ever-changing, increasingly difficult, and demanding. Sometimes, doctors tell us we just need medication in order to cope with life when, in reality, we may *also* need to evaluate the cause of stress in our lives and work to remedy that—instead of simply masking the symptoms.

Pills, alcohol, and other forms of artificial "calming devices" can often do more harm than good. According to a Harvard University Medical School study,[3] about one in every ten Americans takes anti-depressants. Since 1994 and 2008, the use of anti-depressants by teens (twelve years and older) and adults has increased by *400 percent*. Why is this trend becoming reality for the millions of people using prescription medication for anxiety and depression? Well, there are lots of reasons.

THE SUPERHERO SYNDROME

Humans have an inherent desire to do well and to be liked. While this desire is normal, it can lead us down the wrong path as we try (and sometimes fail) to meet others' expectations. Ultimately, the constant striving creates a downward spiral effect—which leaves us wanting immediate relief when failure becomes inevitable.

What happens next is even more tragic. The more we fail, the harder we try. Then when we think that we cannot do things alone under the auspices of our own non-medicated brain and body, we lean toward anything that might provide a calming effect. As consumption increases, dependency increases, and we are left self-medicating to stop any and all pain from taking its toll on our lives. But this circular logic obviously does more harm than good.

Your adversaries don't care if you can cope with things or not. No, they are not going to stop. Their attacks on you may become even more personalized if they are aware of your anxiety and tendency for self-inflicted pressure. From Darlene Murphy's story, which we presented at the start of this chapter, it is evident

---

3   Wehrwein, Peter. "Astounding increase in antidepressant use by Americans." Harvard Health Publications. http://www.health.harvard.edu/blog/astounding-increase-in-antidepressant-use-by-americans-201110203624 (accessed December 7, 2016).

that the use of artificial coping mechanisms increased in relation to the stress she felt. Did her adversaries *make* her take pills and drink? No, of course not. Did Darlene's self-esteem turn jagged as a result of expectations and pressure that were beyond her control? Certainly.

We often become our own worst enemies when we face our toughest battles. This is when we feel the pressure to be *perfect*. We call this the Superhero Syndrome. If we aren't perfect, we psychologically feel like our adversaries will come after us because we are now prone to being perceived as weak. We hand over the flag well before it is close to being captured. Take a look at how Mary's own Superhero Syndrome affected her life:

> *I looked like a bus ran over me—with all four tires. Everyone knew I was stressed out at work. They had to know I was drinking, too. I smelled like a bottle of stale whisky even when I wasn't drinking. I hated my job, hated my life, and hated my colleagues. They ran me into the ground. I think they felt threatened by me. I was the star principal. I was a superhero. So I changed a few test papers. Not a lot. Only a few. I had to keep up my reputation.*
>
> *But cheating was stupid, I know.*
>
> *I went to rehab to grab hold of my alcoholism after I was investigated for cheating on the state tests. It was good that I sought help. I haven't had a drink in three months, but I don't have a job either. I can't get one person to look at my résumé because I will always be labeled as a cheater. My career is ruined. But I'm going to keep trying. If I let this one mistake, this one job, ruin me then I'm worse off than before. What was this all worth? My career-life I guess. I'm glad to be out of there, but the scars are still very fresh.*

I wish I didn't mess up, but I did and now it is costing me my career, being able to support my family, my pension, and my life passion for working with students. I have to have faith in order to grow, so I guess that isn't a bad thing.

I've learned so much from this awful experience. I know that I'm now a better school leader than before. I'm very appreciative of this dunk tank book so it can help other school leaders, whether they are having a hard time in their careers or not. Something can always peek around the corner for even the best school leader out there; and if they don't know how to handle it, they do something out of character as a result.

—MARY WENDOVER,
FORMER PRINCIPAL, ARKANSAS

Mary is cognizant of the contributions she made to her downfall. She took responsibility for her actions and her health. Now, as she struggles to move forward and recognizes "what's over is over," Mary's greatest life lesson is her realization that this one life event should not break her spirit. She victimized herself into thinking that perfection was her only goal.

Mary also knows now that her own superhero mentality was useless in the effort to survive in her career. Her leadership wasn't under attack. In fact, it was just the opposite. Mary carried the weight of the world on her shoulders trying to be perfect. The best test scores. The best staff. Liked by all. If you need something done, give it to Mary. Call Mary: She will have the answers. Enroll your child in Mary's school. She is the best. The very best of the best. In essence, Mary created the adversarial conditions because of unreasonable, self-imposed expectations for perfection.

Her own adversarial mindset, the Superhero Syndrome, pushed her toward perfectionism, drinking, and ultimately, cheating. She ended up trading away her livelihood when she became a drunken superhero. Whiskey consumption was imperfect, but it allowed Mary to cope with trying to be perfect—at least it did for the short term. Now that she's healthy again, she realizes she must maintain a spirit of positivity. Otherwise, she will ultimately lose everything—without adversarial attacks to blame this time.

I don't believe people die from hard work.
They die from stress, worry, and fear.
—A. L. WILLIAMS

WORKPLACE STRESS AND THE CIRCLE OF FEAR

From our research for this book, we found that unreasonable job demands rank among one of the top five reasons for workplace stress. Job insecurity is another.

Earlier, we discussed how fear directs most of the emotional drivers that lead to adversarial turmoil. What is interesting to note is that the fear of losing one's job is a primary emotion of those who face workplace stress (and even adversarial conditions). Often it is this fear of losing one's job or rank that becomes the internalized rationale for adopting harmful, stress-coping behaviors.

Fear, then, is two-fold. Adversaries are driven by self-esteem issues related to the fear of *something*, and their victims' response to their attacks is also driven by fear. The most difficult part about analyzing workplace stress has to do with determining which stressors are external and which might be the result of our own unhealthy mindsets or choices. Sometimes, our "saboteurs," as coined by Durre (2010),[4] lead us down stressful paths. Other times, our own failed coping mechanisms inhibit our progress and potential success.

A myth exists that politics do not exist in school settings. Its sister-fallacy is that, because we are in the business of working with children, adult misbehavior is minimal in the field of education. When educators talk about their own workplace stress, the focus is on managing violent or challenging students or figuring out the best classroom-management techniques. Consider the story of Darius Jacobs, a failed superintendent who became an alcoholic as a result of both a toxic school system environment and Superhero Syndrome as he was rallied by his community, school staff, and other colleagues to fix his school district's problems—or risk losing his job:

I couldn't hold it together. I couldn't. My own legal team was working against me on the inside. Teachers were strategically reporting back to a few poisoned pills on the board who were trying to get their family members and friends back into the district after previously being let go. Board elections were hostile.

Good people were not given tenure because of revenge. I had stacks and stacks of legal papers on my desk. I couldn't do any normal superintendent leadership stuff. It was all about trying to keep this toxic ring of seven or eight people from doing more and more damage to the district. I was beyond stressed out. I was medicated to the point that I was a zombie, just trying to get through each day. I remember praying to God to "get me out of there." But

---

4   Durre, Linnda. *Surviving the Toxic Workplace: Protect Yourself against Coworkers, Bosses, and Work Environments That Poison Your Day.* McGraw-Hill, 2010.

the booze took over. It crippled me. All I wanted to do was drink and not deal with any more garbage.

The staff and community rallied behind me. They told me that if anyone could fix things, I could. I started believing them. My head grew larger and larger. I was going to save that district from these toxic people.

But I didn't. I crashed and burned.

When push came to shove, no one helped me. Not my own local educational officials. Not even the Commissioner of State Education. No one. No returned phone calls from any of them. I asked for help. Hell, I even had lunch with a few officials and asked them for help. No one cared. I mean, they said they cared, but they didn't do anything to really help me.

Then, I crashed. I couldn't take it any longer. I checked into a hospital and got some real help with my alcoholism. I was good at what I did, but the chaos got the best of me. I'll never forget how I was always being followed, how my family was being followed, and how my kids were being videotaped. I remember the cars parked at the corners of the administration building with people watching me travel from school to school on my daily visitations. Whenever I called the police, the mysterious cars would be gone just in time. They knew what they were doing to break me. The bullying. The physical confrontations. All of it. They were good at making my life miserable.

—DARIUS JACOBS,
FORMER SUPERINTENDENT, MARYLAND

Notice the various adversarial, emotional driving forces and tactics used against Darius by his teachers, board members, and legal team. He had to fight the pressures of litigation on a daily basis. Darius can no longer work in public education because of his mistakes and failures—in spite of his remediation and sobriety for sixteen months. He is saddened by the total loss of a highly successful career in education. Public education isn't an option for him. He comes with too much baggage and bad press, even though no one truly knows the real story behind his downfall and what he really went through.

We met up with Darius a few months after our interview and learned that he found work as an assistant director at a learning center a few miles from his house. He is doing well and even joked with us about "all the money that he saves each week by not drinking." He works with kids and parents on how to best support children who are struggling readers. He is happy, relieved, and prevailing in his career even though it isn't in a public school setting.

Be willing to change your circumstances; don't settle for the temporary stress relief with pills or alcohol. This profession is amazing. It can also be amazingly difficult and stressful. When the going gets tough, there are all kinds of paths you can take. Some school leaders head down paths of destruction. You don't have to go that way. You have supporters all around you who are willing to help you find a better, healthier path. The reality is, we all need a little help now and again to get back on track. The question for each one of us is this: *Can we admit it?*

I start with the premise that the function of leadership is to produce more leaders, not more followers.

—**Ralph Nader**

CHAPTER 7

Gathering Allies

THINK OF ANY WAR that has ever happened or that is going on today. What do all of those wars have in common? They all have armies or, at the very least, alliances that give them the potential for victory. Would General Lee have entered the battlefield alone without a Confederate army behind him? Of course not. It is a silly concept, battling alone. So why should we try to tackle dunk tank conditions alone?

The wars you must fight in your career cannot and should not ever be fought alone. In this chapter you will learn where to find allies and how to build the relationships and create the circumstances to grow your army. Consider this story first:

My colleagues and I were so sad to see him retire; after all, he was one of the best principals we had ever worked alongside. He was stealth-like in the way that he created leaders.

Principal Stan Sterling was always looking for opportunities to build and test leadership skills. I can remember the year we hired a new teacher to our faculty; she was a third-year teacher and, right away, exhibited excellent classroom management, strong rapport among staff and students, and effective teaching far beyond her years of experience. Stan wanted to test the waters to see if Miss Stefani was ready to become a teacher-leader without placing her in a full-fledged leadership role, and he did this without anyone knowing that she was on his radar. He wanted the opportunity to groom her in case she lacked any of the necessary skills to lead adults.

Principal Sterling was notorious for "making up" jobs, community events, or committees just for the sake of building leaders. Since he wanted to groom Miss Stefani for a future leadership role, he called her into his office one day and said, "Miss Stefani, I was thinking about having some type of community event here at school where we can invite parents in and get them more involved with math. I've been in your classroom and have seen the math fluency games that you have set up in your stations and how your students have effectively implemented math interactive notebooks. Your kids are really showing great improvement in their benchmark data, and they just love math time in your class. I was wondering if you could help me with planning a curriculum night about math fluency that parents could support their students with at home. I would like to take what you do in your classroom and turn it into a parent night so we can make a positive impact on even more kids. I believe that every student in our school deserves to experience the same success that your kids experience in your classroom. Is this something that you could help me with?"

Of course, Miss Stefani was extremely proud and so flattered that she couldn't turn down this opportunity to support her principal and the students at her school.

—JOSE GONZALEZ,
INSTRUCTIONAL COACH, ILLINOIS

This is a perfect example of positive aligned relatedness. Principal Sterling intentionally built an alliance with Miss Stefani. There was a perceived common agreement and an aligned mindset. If he had approached this differently, the outcome may not have been what he desired. For example, if he had called Miss Stefani into his office and said, "We have a curriculum night coming up, and I want you to run it for me," it may have been perceived as one more thing to do, or possibly even a punishment. But in this case, the principal was strategically building a leader. Listen to what Stan Sterling had to say when we followed up with him:

I knew that Miss Stefani was a top-notch teacher; what I didn't know was if her skills would transfer over to influencing her peers and the community. I also wanted to test her natural instincts for making solid decisions as well as her organization and ability to meet timelines. We did have a curriculum night allotted on the year-long calendar, but it was very flexible.

I specifically turned this into a scenario that forced Miss Stefani and I to work closely together to carry out this school-wide event. She was so excited that she came back to my office the following day with classroom rotation ideas. She even had the idea to hand out stamp cards to encourage participation. She was organized and ready with a map and the logistics on how the evening would flow and had identified the type of support we would need from various stakeholders. She really put her heart and soul into creating this event.

This was an opportunity for me to see her level of self-initiative and her organization and passion while stepping up. I was able to ask leading questions to get her to consider a letter that would need to go home to parents, post on social media, support our teachers, and get kids excited to come.

She returned to my office the next day with a rough draft letter to be sent home and had the idea of putting together a student commercial and having the National Junior Honor Society make posters and sponsor prizes if students came and completed their punch cards. We revised the letter together with wording that needed to be considered, and I played off of her excitement for marketing to the community, students, parents, and teachers.

Next, I shared that involving community volunteers would also make a positive impact. I volunteered to reach out to our local Kiwanis club and roster of retirees that volunteer. We worked together with much collaboration. She and I even co-facilitated some professional development opportunities to support our teachers on math fluency games and interactive student notebooks.

Miss Stefani rose to the occasion, just as I had suspected, and I was able to coach her on communication, facilitating professional development, marketing, and community

*involvement. It was a win-win situation for both of us,
and now I know that I can continue grooming her for a
teacher-leader role in the near future.*

—*STAN STERLING,
PRINCIPAL, KENTUCKY*

If Principal Sterling had never sought out this alliance and
provided an opportunity to groom Miss Stefani as a teacher
leader, it would have been a missed opportunity to capitalize on
the notion of positive aligned relatedness. In this scenario, Principal Sterling was an effective leader creating a positive climate
and, more importantly, creating another leader. During a staff
meeting that followed the event, Stan gave Miss Stefani kudos
and specific praise by thanking her. Principal Sterling was the
epitome of a true leader.

GATHERING ALLIES FROM UNLIKE GROUPS

Gathering allies can help us all thrive in a positive climate
and will empower us to prevail in the school leader's dunk tank.
Understanding layers of influence, emotional intelligence, and
relationship inter-connectedness can make or break any of us.

The law of attraction states that "like will attract like." This
natural occurrence is different from the Hollywood idea that
"opposites attract." While that may work in the movies—and
perhaps in personal relationships—in our professional lives, we
naturally gravitate toward people who are similar to us, those
who put us at ease.

The people with whom we surround ourselves influence
who we become. So it makes sense that we should want to be
influenced by nice people—people who encourage us to be
our best and challenge us to think objectively. As you look for

alliances, finding the right people matters; finding nice people matters even more. The more positive relationships you have, the greater your circle of influence will become. It is this circle of influence—your alliances—that greatly impacts your ability to navigate the pitfalls and obstacles that come with any leadership position.

But remember, as you look for the knowledge, skills, and attitudes of those with whom you wish to align yourself, consider their abilities for completing tasks *and* for supporting and insulating your leadership goals.

Gathering allies will help you to do the following:

1. Preserve your own happiness

2. Preserve your own moral compass

3. Make intentional and solid decisions

4. Stay current in your practices and relevant to others

5. Reflect on your own behaviors and schema

6. Focus on outcomes and goals

7. Navigate the school leader's dunk tank

BUILDING ALLIES

Great minds discuss ideas; average minds discuss events; small minds discuss people.
—ELEANOR ROOSEVELT

Building alliances may start out feeling awkward, scripted, or uncomfortable. The following five nexus groups link who you are with who you will become throughout your professional journey. Creating these relationships will require focus and reflection as you expand your boundaries and gather more allies.

As we discussed, fear is a powerful underlying emotional driver. You may feel fearful about making new alliances. That's natural. People have always had a fear of the unknown, a fear of how they will be received, and a fear of what others may think. The reality is, it will take time and practice before the act of reaching out and building new relationships feels normal. With a strategic plan and approach, you will discover over time that building alliances can become second nature. Even better, these relationships will become authentic connections. Alliance building within each of these nexus groups will require perseverance and intentional dedication to people. Starting with those inside your organization, the ideals of vertical relationships fit well with our study of dunk tank survival.

VERTICAL RELATIONSHIPS

Vertical relationships are relationships with people within your direct organization with whom you work on a daily basis. This includes your direct supervisor (or a higher rank) on your district's organizational chart. It also includes the people who support you, such as an administrative assistant, aide, crossing guard, instructional coach, dean, principal, coordinator, director, executive team member, superintendent, school board member, and so on. This is probably the most difficult type of relationship to nurture because these are the people whom you want to please most and with whom you work most closely. They are also the ones who may very well have control over your job success and evaluation. They are the people at the epicenter of the work that you do.

The people comprising this group may also be the cause of the most angst or anxiety and may have their own intentions of placing you in the dunk tank. Remember that within this group, anyone within your department may be controlling the school leader's dunk tank. Keep your "proactive paranoia" intact. Be watchful for those people who may be in search of materialized leadership symbolism (while also showing it off). In the following story, a principal experienced the realities of how negative vertical relationships can lead to public humiliation:

> We had monthly, combined administrator meetings run by Sue, our superintendent. At first, things were calm. Then September rolled around.
>
> Sue would use scenarios from our schools of how not to do things, name us, call us out, and then basically neuter us in front of our peers. She crushed me at one particular meeting, saying that one of my teachers provided too much information to a student she was administering a state assessment to. As a result, we had to report it and we were cited because of it. I didn't fail to train my teachers on exam administration ethics and guidelines, but I was bashed for not doing it the right way.
>
> I tried to miss a few meetings by making sure I had something else to do in my own life so I could take a sick day, but that didn't matter. My colleagues told me that Sue talked about some of the things that I allegedly did even when I was absent.
>
> Sue made sure that during her meetings she had a tall, high-back leather business chair while we all sat on some low-seated stacking chairs. She was in control, and she wanted us to know it on every level. How was I supposed to get Sue to be an ally when she kicked my butt all over the place during her meetings?

I wasn't the only one, either, so I think it didn't have to do only with me. Sue just didn't really like anyone.

—Jim Crawford,
Principal, Louisiana

While the high-back leather chair epitomized materialized leadership symbolism and a self-importance that Sue was trying to display, it appeared that she didn't necessarily *dislike* Jim. This was how she operated with everyone around her. While Jim exercised "proactive paranoia" prior to these types of signs or events, Jim was in a perfect place to reposition himself. He could investigate whether he could pursue a vertically aligned relationship with his direct supervisor as an ally.

Creating positive vertical relationships might help Jim to prevail in his career, regardless of whether Sue truly wants to see him drown or if she is just asserting her materialized leadership symbolism and flashing her peacock feathers. Simple gestures like those that follow could help him (and you) establish more positive connections with others:

- **Note the small things.** Remember his/her favorite sports teams, preferences, alma-mater, anything unrelated to your organization that will create a conversation starter the next time you see them. Use it to create personable, common associations that have nothing to do with work. Be observant. These may help initiate positive interactions that may lead you into positive aligned actions. We are not recommending kissing up or brown-nosing. That is different, and you can tell the difference.

- **Volunteer.** Offer to help on a project or to cover for someone who is out of the office. Look for opportunities to be helpful. Make your helpfulness professionally relevant, not artificial (e.g., setting up a committee to examine an issue that has repeatedly surfaced versus getting a plate of food for your supervisor during a holiday gathering). The latter will only create more dissent as it will be looked upon as seeking favoritism.

- **Brag on a colleague.** The biggest compliment you can give a leader is complimenting someone he/ she leads. And if the word gets back to the person being complimented, your effort is doubly effective. Secondhand compliments carry a lot of weight. Compliment and recognize good work even if the good work is coming from an adversary.

- **Write notes.** Leave a handwritten card or sticky note with positive sayings or messages related to a common goal. Be thoughtful. Be strategic. Don't be gaudy or sappy. Keep these professionally relevant as well.

- **Read body language.** If you can sense that someone is having a bad day or something is off, offer emotional support and extend understanding. Show compassion. Listen empathetically. Validate. Support.

HORIZONTAL RELATIONSHIPS

As you move through the hierarchy of recognizing potential adversaries or working to cope alongside those who do not show you any respect, the next level of your relationship-building is horizontal. Horizontal relationships include the people in your peer group. If you are a superintendent, your horizontal group consists of your fellow superintendents. If you are a principal, your horizontal relationships are your principal colleagues within the district. These relationships are oftentimes the most relatable connections because you face similar situations and obstacles and have comparable expertise and professional experiences. Here are some entry points for creating positive horizontal relationships:

- **Send an e-mail**. Share an encouraging quote, relevant current happenings, or a link to an inspirational video that is relevant to your common work. Be an *encourager*.

- **Share ideas**. As projects are given out and due dates are set, touch base with the people in this group to see if they could use support with the process. Be *collaborative*.

- **Publically compliment**. If you notice someone in this group who makes an impact on others, or goes above and beyond, jot it down and share it at your next group meeting.

- **Send an encouraging note**. Periodically send your colleagues a note of encouragement through inter-office district mail. It could be serious or silly as long as it is thoughtful. Make it *personal*.

- **Share resources**. If you know one of your colleagues is working on a specific initiative and you have experience or resources, such as research articles, presentations, or books, share them on loan.

COMMUNITY RELATIONSHIPS

Now is the time to look outside for other ally power. Your community is overwhelmingly influential. Go after them and build your army. Community relationships include parents, parent-teacher associations, community voters, teacher associations, other community stakeholders, and business partners. This group of allies is one of the most important nexus groups of allies, but it is often added to an invitation list late in the game or even as an afterthought. In reality, this is one of the most important groups of allies because they have enormous influence over what happens in their schools. They will question what doesn't seem right, and they will rise up to speak their minds about adversarial conditions, the adversaries themselves, and about issues that need fixing. After all, they have nothing to lose, so they can be very supportive of your efforts if you need allies to help you through tough times.

However, you must be sure that your efforts to build these relationships are noble. Never succumb to backstabbing or any negative behavior that could diminish your positive-role-model status. Likewise, make sure these relationships never interfere with your ability to stay focused on student achievement, staff growth, and student and staff happiness. It is when you are true to yourself, to your students, and to your staff that the community will rally behind. Ryan Abrahamsen shares how his community relationships supported him in his third year as a principal:

My superintendent thought I was OK. The board hated me, though. They thought I was too soft with my school discipline. But my parents loved me. I worked so closely with them. They thought I was fair. They knew I loved kids. I think the board wanted me gone, and they knew my tenure vote was coming up in a couple of months. Out of nowhere, my superintendent gave me a poor evaluation. I think he felt the pressure to please his board so his own job wasn't on the line. He gave in and wrote a terrible evaluation to keep his own nose clean.

While talking to my PTA president one day, I confided in her since we are friends and work so closely together. We think the same: It's all for the kids. Well, when the parents got word of what was going on, suddenly an army of them came to the board meetings and spoke during the public session about how awesome I was. When it came to tenure vote time, the board had no choice but to approve my tenure or they would have had a community mutiny on their hands. Did I actively try to use parents for my own gain? No. Did this accidentally happen? Yes. Could it be a strategy for those in the dunk tank down the road? Only if you are true to yourself and are worth fighting for.

—RYAN ABRAHAMSEN,
K–5 PRINCIPAL, MISSOURI

Here, a dunk tank tool in the career-protective tool box emerges. While community supporters could clearly rise up to fight for a school leader—regardless of whether they are actively or passively sought out by the dunk tank victim—Ryan makes a powerful point. They'll only show up "if you are worth fighting for." Poor performers rarely receive sweeping community support. It is when you are making good decisions for children and adults that you can garner solid community support. If you are feeble, unskilled, power hungry, or complacent, you cannot expect your recruited allies to step up and defend you—no matter how "right" you think you are.

The following basic entry points for creating positive community relationships can help you in the long run. More importantly, they should be infused into your daily method of operation anyway since they are best practices for working with other people:

- **Attend all school board meetings**. Being seen at public forums shows your personal investment in the organization. Smile, shake hands, and get to know people sitting around you.

- **Attend as many afterschool events as possible**. Parents are one of the biggest assets in schools today. Get to know the people in your school community who are invested in your kids. Smile, shake hands, and make connections.

- **Write thank you notes**. Anytime you have a business partner or community member volunteer or provide a service, e-mail or send a card and make them feel like they are an appreciated part of your school.

- **Introduce yourself, constantly**. Introverts who are summoned to the dunk tank rarely prevail. Anytime you encounter someone new in your building, walk up and smile, shake their hand, and let them know you appreciate them being there.

- **Invite all in, always**. Invite as many community partners, associations, and stakeholders as possible to share a new learning method, skill, or information that would make an impact on your group. Create opportunities and celebration days to extend an invitation to engage with everyone.

- **Ask for representation on committees that you are running**. Your adversaries will make sure that they sit in on committees or meetings where you are and are not present. They will seek to have representation in all areas of the school or district so they can continue to create adversarial campaigns. So get your team or allies assembled and step up to the scrimmage line.

- **Don't be absent or late, ever**. We all get sick. We all have family tragedies or difficulties that demand our attention. But sometimes, we just want to avoid possibly controversial situations. Maybe you get a sick feeling in your stomach when you think about attending a certain meeting. Maybe the thought of seeing your adversary's face makes you want to show up late and hide in the back row. Get past it. If you are late or absent, your adversaries will use it to their advantage. They strive to get their own negative aligned relatedness on each and every committee that makes recommendations or decisions for the district, and those decisions might come back to haunt you. If you are present, you have a much better chance at stopping bad decisions. At a minimum, you will be able to publically voice your concerns and allow your community to hear your side of the story.

EXTERNAL PROFESSIONAL RELATIONSHIPS

Your regional fellows might also be a community relationship, but if they are not, a whole other world of allies can assist with your dunk tank struggles. These are referred to as external professional relationships. External professional relationships include the colleagues that you meet at conferences, the ones with whom you connect through various organizations, those in your LinkedIn network, or even the ones you meet up with in other technological groups or follow on blogs. These are positive leaders. These are the "smart" people you intentionally place in your life and surround yourself with as influencers. These are your Twitter chat crewmembers. You may find initiating new relationships with this group to be most intimidating as they may have more experience and more knowledge, and are considered experts and highly successful in their organization. Check out this story from Rick (the co-author of this book) about the outcome of a connection he made with another professional he admired:

> I've always admired Todd Whitaker. I remember listening to him speak when I attended a conference as a principal. He is down-to-earth, practical, and thoughtful. He has tons of experience, is a great author on leadership, and is really just a great guy. I even remembered him to be highly entertaining and funny when I saw him

in person. I read a couple of his books, and they kept me going in my career as a principal at the time.

I reached out to Todd on LinkedIn and gave him a generic connection request. He accepted it a few weeks later. I didn't do much with this new professional relationship for quite a while. I mean, even though I knew him, I was a stranger to him. I was just glad to see some of his posts and other stuff.

A few months later, something really cool happened. After I accepted my first book deal with Routledge, I noticed that Todd had a ton of stuff published by them too. I wanted to learn more about what my experience with Routledge would be like, so I thought I would drop him a message and ask for some advice.

In a couple of days, he responded to my message and told me to call him whenever I needed anything. We talked about book writing, deciding on a cover design, and solving real problems in education. He was amazing to chat with. He wasn't conceited like some other big names in education who won't even take a minute to shake your hand. A few months later, after a couple more phone conversations and messages back and forth, Todd wrote an endorsement for my first book, Hiring the Best Staff for Your School.

I still chat with him for advice and mentorship. Most recently, he praised the work that Dave Burgess was doing, and as a result, I reached out to Dave and Paul Solarz regarding their incredible Pirate series books. I contacted Paul on Twitter and we spoke a day later. Nice guy. Smart too. So helpful.

I consider all of my connections professional friends. It's even so amazing how Rebecca and I became acquainted and then decided to co-author this book, but that is a whole other story that can be found on our website.

Being intentional can lead to unimaginable successes. The power of professional relationships is that they can help you prevail in dunk tank situations *and* help you craft big dreams. Social media is a powerful force across so many industries—education included. Cultivating these kinds of relationships requires you to do a few things:

- **Connect on social media, always**. Put yourself out there. Join LinkedIn and Twitter and start connecting with like-minded colleagues who have similar professional interests. Connect with professional organizations and read their newsfeeds and articles. Watch their video clips. Comment on the posts that most impact or influence you. This will begin a collegial dialogue thread and may lead to more professional relationships.

- **Attend trainings, constantly**. While attending professional state-wide and vendor trainings, network with other professionals. Leverage your time expanding your network. Introduce yourself. Sit with someone new. Trade business cards. Remember, introverted leadership won't give you water wings in the dunk tank.

- **Follow blogs and comment regularly**. Focus on a relevant topic and new learning. Select a blog to follow. Read. Comment. Reply. Repeat. It's time consuming, we know, but you will grow in new and amazing ways.

- **Join professional organizations ASAP**. Find local, state, and national organizations that focus on your key learning areas, beliefs, or topics. Read journals, watch webinars, and attend locally sponsored events. Crave new knowledge. You will stumble upon so many things that will help you to survive and thrive.

- **Attend webinars, Google hangouts, or Skype sessions**. Take time to routinely watch a live video-stream, interact on a Google hangout or teleconference, post comments, interact, and ask questions. Exchange personal information and send follow-up e-mail questions, and leverage resource sharing. Remember, social media is just that: social, not anti-social.

Your external professional relationships will build you up and never tear you down. They can also counteract your dunk tank life in incredible ways. This is part of the plan that we have put together for you to prevail in your career even when you are among chaotic climates. Professional relationships can start out as generic or impersonal, but when nurtured, they have the potential to grow into powerful, personal relationships.

PERSONAL RELATIONSHIPS

Personal relationships include the people in your life with whom you may have a long history, are employed outside of your workplace, or share similar interests, age, culture, nationality, ideology, religion, or backgrounds. These are your go-to people for emotional support. You are most comfortable with this ally group and are most likely to go to them and ask for help. They are your "phone-a-friend' confidants. Consider this story from Christopher Reinhart, a former superintendent of schools in New Jersey, and how his personal relationship with another superintendent helped him to navigate making a correct decision when faced with extreme adversity:

I really didn't know what to do. We all know that new contract negotiations want new money and fresh raises, and I knew that I wouldn't be able to tackle getting all of the bargaining units to concede—especially since they were mad at me for last year's layoffs. So I called my buddy, Kevin, just to get a clear head. When I talked to him, he was great. He told me what he was doing in his district. All of his administrators took a $5,000 pay cut if the unions would concede to a half-step increase instead of a full-step increase on their salary schedules.

When the bargaining units saw a freeze for all administrators and a pay cut, they started to listen. They didn't like what was in store for them, but they at least took us seriously. When we had some meaningful discussions, they saw that the list of twenty-eight layoffs for this year would go away if they considered a half-step increase. We led by example. We started the conversations. We tried it.

The result: We saved everyone's jobs and class sizes didn't get crazy. I never thought about a half-step increment. It's so simple; yet, it didn't cross my mind. If I didn't call Kevin, I wouldn't have gotten the unions to collaborate with me and come to this concession. Now, I owe Kevin dinner and a few beers. That's the least I can do for how things turned out. I couldn't sleep. It was really killing me.

—CHRISTOPHER REINHART,
SUPERINTENDENT, NEW JERSEY

Here, Christopher "phoned his friend" Kevin and gained insights into some difficult and turbulent times in his district. Some basic entry points for turning professional connections into positive personal relationships that can help you with your struggles might include the following:

- **Meet for an activity**. Most likely, you are connected by a common interest and meet to do things outside of work. If you meet someone in one of the other ally groups with whom you share a connection and common interest, you may want to meet outside of work time for recreation or just simply for a meal.

- **Text**. One of the easiest ways to stay personally connected is through short, positive, encouraging text messages or to communicate events and happenings.

- **Call**. When you need support, or you know someone else is going through something more challenging than normal, pick up the phone and call. Communicating voice to voice is still the one of the best ways to connect.

- **Celebrate events**. Holidays, birthdays, and special celebrations are important. From silly decorations to more meaningful thank-you sentiments, a cupcake or cup of coffee can make all the difference and make people feel loved.

- **Encourage**. You know your friends best. Be in tune and support them through conversation, thoughtfulness, dinner, or a note of encouragement. Be there for them because the dunk tank is not isolated to only you. You may have a lot in common, and your strategies for moving forward and jumping over barriers may work better with a partner.

Gathering allies and expanding your circle of influence is all about creating common ground, nurturing, and growing new relationships. Each of these groups range on a continuum of comfort and proximity, both socially and professionally. Each person has a different threshold for interactive social tolerance outside their comfort zone. It takes courage to initiate each of these nexus group relationships, but it is worth it.

ALLIANCE-BUILDING ACTIONS

We all want to work in an extraordinary workplace, for an exceptional leader, without internal or external dunk tank scenarios facing us. But those kinds of circumstances occur by happenstance. Sometimes it doesn't happen at all. You may have experienced failure in turning adversaries into allies in the past. When you are faced with adversarial conditions, it is time to take action.

When a positive work culture does not exist, allies become an even more precious commodity. You will want to guard yourself against your adversaries while taking action to gather more allies. Your allies will help you to be prepared with how you will respond, how you will act, what you will say, and how you should lead from within. It is time to follow your healthy "proactive paranoia" with preparedness and a mindset for battle by gathering up your allies and taking action. These actions will aide you as you gather up like-minded allies who have your best interest in mind.

SEEK OUT EMOTIONALLY INTELLIGENT PEOPLE

Anyone can become angry. That is easy. But to be angry with the right person, to the right degree, at the right time, for the right purpose, and in the right way: that is not easy.

—Aristotle

There is power and strength in numbers. Surround yourself with emotionally intelligent people. These are people who have a self-awareness of their own emotions and are able to handle interpersonal relationships judiciously and empathetically. They recognize their own triggers and stressors; they know their emotional limits. Emotionally intelligent people have the ability to self-regulate their emotions according to situations while positively impacting those around them.

We recommend surrounding yourself with those who have high Emotional Intelligence (EQ). Dunk tank situations can take a toll on emotionally strong school leaders. When fear takes over or when survival feels impossible, our brain's amygdala, a mass of cells within the limbic system, governs our emotions, motivations, muscles, and senses. It is here that our brain determines whether to fight or flee.

People with a high EQ are able to . . .

- listen to their emotions
- read non-verbal cues and body language
- incorporate humor with good timing
- resolve conflict appropriately
- demonstrate resiliency
- show positive self-regard as it pertains to their strengths and weaknesses
- adapt
- assert themselves
- be flexible
- problem solve
- demonstrate impulse control
- manage stress

- exude happiness and optimism

Take time to take a step back to listen, observe, and gravitate towards people who demonstrate these characteristics. These are the people to seek out and embrace. They will give you the advantage of multiple perspectives on even the most hostile issue.

BUILD TRUST

Men of genius are admired, men of wealth
are envied, men of power are feared, but
only men of character are trusted.
—Zig Ziglar

We've heard this all before. Trust is one of the most written-about leadership characteristics because it points to so many things all at once: reliability, truth, legitimacy, and ability. As humans, we have a natural disposition to judge a person's trustworthiness. What this means for us as we gather allies is that we are constantly being judged and either deemed trustworthy—or not. Trust is not only about relationships and entrusting someone with confidential information; it is also about following through with commitments, timelines, and agreements.

The lasting effects of broken trust can be detrimental to a school leader's career before, during, or after dunk tank failure or survival. Establishing and maintaining trust through every step is the key to building positive, thriving alliances.

DISPLAY DISCERNMENT

*Discernment is not
knowing the difference
between right and wrong.
It is knowing the difference
between right and almost right.*

—C. H. Spurgeon

Discernment is the ability to judge well. Allies with a strong sense of discernment will serve you very well as they help you preserve your own happiness and moral compass. You will need to put on your dunk tank *with-it-ness* goggles to watch for allies who exhibit these qualities. In Anthony Bryk and Barbara Schneider's book, *Trust in Schools,*[5] they identify four criteria for trust *discernment*, which are listed below:

1. **Respect**

   Respect involves recognition of the important role that each person plays in a child's education and the mutual dependencies that exist among various parties involved in this activity.

2. **Competence**

   Competence is the ability to achieve desired outcomes, to include not only learning objectives for children, but also effective work conditions for teachers and administrators who need to maintain positive school–community relations.

---

5   Bryk, Anthony S. and Barbara L. Schneider. *Trust in Schools: A Core Resource for Improvement.* New York: Russell Sage Foundation, 2004.

3. Personal Regard for Others

Actions that reduce others' sense of vulnerability affect their interpersonal trust. Interpersonal trust deepens as individuals perceive that others care about them and are willing to extend themselves beyond what their role might formally require in any given situation.

4. Integrity

In our daily social encounters, we think of individuals as having integrity if there is a consistency between what they say and do. Integrity also implies that a moral-ethical perspective guides one's work.

Just as you are looking for future allies that display discernment, your display of discernment across all of your nexus groups will cultivate new followers.

USE NON-VIOLENT COMMUNICATION

*Wise men talk because
they have something to say;
fools talk because they
have to say something.*
—PLATO

Believe it or not, peaceful solutions exist for even the most adversarial conditions and situations. Dr. Marshall Rosenberg, founder of the Center for Nonviolent Communication, developed the Nonviolent Communication (NVC) process as a peaceful alternative to violence. He identifies four components to NVC as a process to a structured conversation. We want to share these with you since they are pertinent to the skills you'll need to cultivate for surviving dunk tank conditions:

1. *Observations*—the concrete actions we observe that affect our well-being

2. *Feelings*—how we feel in relation to what we observe

3. *Needs*—the needs, values, desires, etc. that create our feelings

4. *Requests*—the concrete actions we request in order to enrich our lives

Let's take a look back at the scenario in Chapter 1 when Sylvia Anderson demonstrated "proactive paranoia." She was worried that her superintendent was overloading her with work in order to bring in one of his best friends. Using the NVC process, Sylvia wrote out how she could approach the superintendent with her concerns:

> *I have noticed that, very recently, you have loaded me up with seven additional projects in a short period of time. I have worked in this district for fourteen years and absolutely adore our staff, and I am proud to be part of this community. Ever since you gave me the additional projects to do on top of my other duties, I have been working fifteen- to sixteen-hour days to try to meet your expectations.*

> *I want to feel successful and meet your expectations. I really do. I have felt like you keep adding to my plate just to find my breaking point. I am highly efficient and I feel like there isn't anyone who could maintain this current*

work load. I want to be supportive of these additional projects and be effective at my regular job duties.

Is it possible to sit down together and look at my list of projects and duties and come up with a plan to accomplish these projects while maintaining some balance in my life? We may even be able to get some others to support these district projects and divide and conquer them for quicker success. I need you to understand how this vicious cycle is impacting the organization, my department, and me personally.

—SYLVIA ANDERSON,
ASSISTANT SUPERINTENDENT, WEST VIRGINIA

Sylvia is already facing an adversarial relationship. A conversation like this could add fuel to the fire, or it may diffuse the situation. Regardless of how her superintendent responds, this approach allows her to maintain her lifelong mantra: "Do what's right and give it your best, because life is the most meaningful test."

In most cases, it is helpful to confront, rather than ignore, a problem that it is causing emotional and physical imbalance in your life. Addressing an issue while it is still small is the ideal approach. The NVC process is highly effective with any audience and any confrontation, whether big or small: acknowledge your feelings, state the facts, and offer a possible solution. Alliance builders use effective communication and have honest conversations to let others know the impact they have on them.

ACCEPT THAT NEPOTISM AND FAVORS EXIST

Some struggle is healthy.
If you can embrace it
rather than be angry,
you can use it as your pilot light.
—**Damon Wayans**

Another action of alliance building is to accept that nepotism and favors will take place within your organization. In many corporate organizations and family-run businesses, nepotism can be praised as a strength, as it brings about commitment, loyalty, and trust while minimizing turnover rates because of a high level of job security. In other cases, nepotism is considered bad because it becomes divisive due to favoritism and power struggles. Regardless, they will always be part of business. So why fight it? Why not embrace it? Why try to control that which is uncontrollable?

One of the keys to surviving the school leader's dunk tank is being realistic enough to accept that things like nepotism and inequity are inevitable. Another key is being objective and having a plan to ride it out. While accepting the reality of nepotism and carrying out favors doesn't necessarily focus on the types of people you need to recruit into your camp of allies, it focuses in on how *not* to buck those who are not your allies. Both strategies are central to your success.

Whether you are in the inner circle of your organization or are failing miserably, you must come to the realization that accepting the circumstance of nepotism and rampant favors is not optional. It has happened and will continue to happen, and it is a factor well out of your control. You will never win going up against this beast. You want to fly under this radar and come out unscathed.

Corrupt people surround themselves with an army of people that will protect them. If you appear unaligned with the troops, then any one of them will purchase a bucket of balls, and the school leader's dunk tank will be initiated. Your goal isn't to get on your adversary's "good side." You don't want recognition or special favors from your adversary. Rather, your goal is to remain neutral.

This is an unjust harsh truth that occurs within school districts. Connecting with ineffective leaders and being kind to your adversaries in a work setting doesn't mean that you are accepting their fear-driven behaviors. It *does* mean that you are accepting them as human beings—people with whom you must connect to keep your organization functioning well. Your actions and response to nepotism and favors will make or break the outcome of your career. This is clearly something that is out of your locus of control and some of the best and brightest school leaders are the ones who insist on trying to have control over that which is uncontrollable.

On the other hand, how you respond to a situation is within the realm of your control. You must rise above the injustice and serve the organization with integrity, regardless of anyone's behaviors.

PLANTING TREES AND GROWING FRUIT

Trees that are slow to grow
bear the best fruit.
—MOLIÈRE

Just as you nurture a seed into a seedling and a seedling into a tree, so you too must nurture and cultivate even your most damaging adversaries. There are several key elements that you will need to consider as you cultivate your new allies while pacifying your adversaries:

1. Kill them with kindness (because you have nothing to lose by planting a seed).

2. Offer positive rumors and secondhand compliments (because sowing is better than destroying).

3. Celebrate and be social but don't inebriate (because one should not overwater a seedling). Keep it classy.

4. Create boundaries (because even trees need fencing sometimes).

5. Confide in someone outside your organization (because sometimes the soil is not fertile in your own backyard garden).

6. Privately document your own positive efforts (because your own trial and errors on cultivation will help you strategize your next planting season).

7. Make connections with everyone even if you have to fake a smile (because talking cruel to a plant will always make it die).

8. Dodge discussing religion, politics, and other people (because sowing these seeds will only lead to the stunted controversial growth of weeds).

Gathering allies is a form of leadership that requires intentional skill and practice over time. Leading takes considerable persistence and patience (and a lot of hours and energy). But remember—this is the greatest job on earth!

Gathering allies among your nexus groups requires heart. The rewards are that you will have the support you need to ensure that you are happy, ethical, intentional, growing, reflecting, and achieving outcome-based goals. Building ally groups is about preserving your own self-worth, guarding self-value, and maintaining a balance in life. Likewise, this support system will help you survive the dunk tank.

A good general not only sees the way to victory; he also knows when victory is impossible.

—POLYBIUS

CHAPTER 8

KNOWING WHEN TO RETREAT

S *he was out to get me, and I knew it. I felt like a failure at creating relationships with the key players at the district office. I worked for Chelsea, the queen of nepotism. My anger flared every time she hired someone from her secret rolodex. I had been able to hide my exasperation and internalize the feelings for quite some time. I knew what she was doing was wrong, but I also knew that she was my boss. All the others seemed to play the game. They told jokes with her sister when she moved into our department, they complimented her best*

friend, and high-fived her nephew when he showed up to do contract work.

Finally, it got to the point that I couldn't stomach it. It was wrong, and I felt like accepting the behavior was a compromise of my own moral ethics. I didn't hang out with them on the weekends drinking, I didn't high five, I didn't tell jokes, and I slowly started to disengage. I wanted no part of that faction so I stayed focused on my work and ignored the antics. No matter how hard I worked, I was always unnoticed and irrelevant to my boss. The value in our department was not on quality research, knowledge, or student achievement; it was on the shenanigans of this corrupt social appendage. Slowly over time, it happened: I became the worker bee and nothing more. I was used for my expertise and disregarded as a person.

At some point, I went from worker bee to adversary without committing any crime and without any warning. After I crossed over to the outer circle of distrust, things really became maddening. Chelsea would no longer look me in the eye, she would get quiet when I walked into a room, and she stopped sending communications and excluded me from attending important meetings. She was getting in my head and emotionally manipulating me. She loaded me up with projects that were an overflow of her executive director level work. She knew I had the expertise and initiative to deliver high-quality work and meet her timelines, so she consistently slid last-minute projects over to me. While she was strolling into work for the day at ten or eleven o'clock, mid-morning, I was slaving away producing her work, for which she would take credit.

To the outside world, the department seemed to be running effectively. Internally, I was flailing, barely surviving. I went home stressed out every night. I had several allies in other departments, but they added fuel to the fire by telling me the lies and misconceptions that Chelsea was spreading about me. I was doing her work, making her look good, and she was out and about ruining my reputation and my good name, all for the sake of her own gain.

My life was spiraling out of control at work. I felt like a social failure and, likewise, I felt trapped in compromising my own beliefs. She even started calling me names in front of my peers. The audacity. The unprofessionalism. I was in a coordinator's meeting and she popped in for a minute and had the nerve to say, "You are so lucky, you have Attila the Hun—that's what we call him." Her behaviors had turned from passive to publically aggressive. It became embarrassing and humiliating.

The straw on the camel's back was the day that I was called into her office and was given a written reprimand. She had written me up for having a lack of confidentiality. Chelsea had spies everywhere. One of her spies had overheard one of my allies talking about my frustrations (all with good intentions), and ratted me out. It was in that moment of being formally reprimanded that I knew my career was doomed and she was out to destroy me. This was the point of no return, and I knew my career in the district was over. She was pushing me out.

—RONNY EDWARDS,
FEDERAL PROGRAMS COORDINATOR, MISSOURI

Like a dropped piece of fine china, sometimes broken things cannot be fixed. Ronny's career had just shattered into a million pieces. It didn't matter that he had integrity. It didn't matter that he cared about the quality of his work and wanted to make a positive impact on the organization. It didn't matter that he went above and beyond. Nothing Ronny did would ever be noticed or recognized because he refused to accept the inevitability of nepotism and favors within his organization. If he'd had on his dunk tank goggles, he may have seen the risks and responded by implementing alliance-building actions such as connecting with and leaning on emotionally intelligent people for advice and establishing trust—both within and outside his office.

In Chapter 2, we discussed Damion's emotional driving force of discrimination and inequality. His need to surround himself with family and friends was a tactic of self-preservation which clearly worked for him. Similarly in this story, Chelsea wasn't out to get Ronny; she was out to preserve the entitlement she had built that allowed her to misbehave. If Ronny had recognized the signs earlier, he would have been able to retreat and intentionally implement a plan to navigate through the injustice while allowing his troop of adversaries to feel less threatened. Keeping the corrupt adversarial troops at bay for as long as possible will buy you time to look for another position. Of course, we aren't blaming Ronny, but using his example may help you understand that identifying emotional driving forces, finding the right allies, and relying on alliance-building skills can help you navigate similar circumstances.

Emotionally intelligent people have the ability to recognize their triggers and stressors and know when it is time to retreat. Clearly, the level of distrust in Chelsea's office, along with the deeply rooted nepotism, triggered emotions in Ronny—emotions that prevented him from stepping back and looking at the situation from multiple perspectives. For example, if he had a rational understanding of Chelsea's emotional driving forces and the adversarial tactics she and her followers used, Ronny might have been able to depersonalize the situation and master the art of dunk tank navigation. Without these dunk tank navigation skills, the human body responds to these threatening situations irrationally.

When faced with a "fight-or-flight" situation, your brain harnesses every possible emotion in the form of nervousness, fear, or full-fledged panic. When you are pushed beyond your comfort zone long term, the stress can damage your mind and body. Recognizing the red flags along the way will help you identify when it is time to wave the white flag or retreat (without thinking of it as quitting) altogether.

RED FLAGS AND WHITE FLAGS

During the honeymoon period of a new job, you are excited about learning all the new processes, procedures, habits, and unspoken rules and norms. And just like those early days of marriage, during this time of job initialization, every stakeholder is on his or her best behavior. Adversarial environments may exist even before you arrive to your new position, but you may not see their effects. That's true, in part, because you are blinded by the rose-colored desire to make a difference. Your intentions are good, and you assume positive intent for those around you. It takes time to learn how to interpret people's habits and behaviors and to make the connection between their actions and true intentions. Consider the story of Jonathan, a principal, who was being approved by a neighboring school district board of education as their new assistant superintendent:

> I didn't resign as principal from my current district until
> I was approved by my new school district's board of education. We all know not to resign from our current position until approved for a new job. So that's what I did.

I drove down to the board meeting with my wife. I was happy to embark on a new assignment in a school district that was highly regarded. I thought: This will be good for my family and my career path.

When I arrived at the board room, the executive session was still going on behind closed doors in the superintendent's office. His office was connected to the board room, however. This wasn't good. You could hear some yelling coming out of the room. One board member was screaming at the superintendent about not wanting to approve me as the new assistant superintendent. She kept yelling at him about my salary recommendation on the board agenda. She was brutal. Then, he called me in so the board could meet me.

It was the weirdest thing I ever sat through. They grilled me with questions, and the board member who had been screaming just stared at me with a laser-beam look that felt like it was going through my skull. As I reflect on these red flags, I shouldn't have taken that job. If I only knew then what I know now, things would have been different. This was a sign that things were only going to get nastier, not better. It wasn't really my salary that upset this board member. It was the war that was already going on between them, and I was going to be guilty by association right from the start. I was the superintendent's new hire, his right-hand guy. So now I was the enemy too. And boy did my life become miserable once I stepped on their soil. I'm no longer in education, but that's another long story.

—JONATHAN BORDEAUX,
FORMER ASSISTANT SUPERINTENDENT, ALABAMA

Retrospect can be painful. For Jonathan, things could have been different if he had heeded the red flags waving during that meeting. He could have declined the approval of his recommendation to become the next assistant superintendent. Would it have upset the superintendent of his new district? Probably. Could it have saved him from the damage done to his career down the road? Maybe. The point is, he had agency in the situation, and had he been aware of adversarial tactics, he might have recognized the warning signs that his new board would likely try to sink him.

You, too, are in control of your own choices. Being mindful of any red flags that may be waving slowly but silently is so crucial. Before taking on a new role, stop. Step back and analyze the situation, and look for and evaluate warning signs *before* making your decision. The same approach applies when you are considering retreat. While escape may be necessary, it should be a last resort, one that comes after you have tried to confront the issues and repair any damage.

Remember, this is your career. You have bills to pay. You have a life and (quite possibly) a family to support. Exerting extra caution and being mindful of any warning flags will help steer you to safer soil. You will need to put on your metaphorical dunk tank goggles and begin watching for validation. Take a look at the red flags that surfaced during our conversations and interviews with people who have experienced the school leader's dunk tank. They may be out of context for your specific circumstances, but they are real stories that illustrate real damage control in education.

Keep an eye out for these red flags so you don't miss them:

- Cliques of individuals excluding new people from their group
- A sixth sense or hunch about something that just isn't right

- Mistruths told by people in aligned groups
- Leading by non-example (do what I say, not what I do)
- The telephone game: You might notice something that you said to someone was spread very quickly and inaccurately through the organization.
- Confiding gossip (I'm not supposed to tell anyone, but . . .)
- Leaders coming late to meetings (repeatedly)
- Colleagues missing deadlines (often)
- Depersonalizing the environment (blatantly)
- Talking about people rather than ideas
- Departments are disconnected (the silo effect)
- Irrelevant policies and/or ignorance of current practices

Watching for these red flags with a strong understanding of the emotional driving forces, adversarial tactics, and the importance of allies, will set you up early enough in the game to steer clear of the dunk tank. These examples are harbingers of dunk tank behaviors. The leadership skill of scanning for red flags is necessary for career survival.

In addition to the covert red flags listed above, overt signs and symptoms may indicate that you have already entered the school leader's dunk tank. If any of these signs and symptoms are already part of your life, you are in the dunk tank zone and may be nearing a point of no return! You must retreat and regroup immediately if any of the following are true for you:

- You are leashed to your cell phone or tablet (a form of non-engagement)
- You receive and send e-mails at all hours of the night

- You work more than ten-hour days
- You seek approval or recognition about anything that you do right
- You are malnourished, are eating on-the-go, or are skipping meals altogether
- You are experiencing anxiety and depression
- You are taking stimulants to stay awake during the day and sedatives to sleep at night
- You are consuming alcohol and pills just to feel normal or stay calm
- You use profanity excessively
- You are operating out of fear
- You are missing dinner and events with your family and loved ones
- You are compromising your own moral or ethical code
- You are retreating from doing anything fun for pleasure
- You are isolating yourself

If any combination of these symptoms is a reality for you, you are headed towards a potential downward spiral. The only way to break this vicious cycle is to stop dead in your tracks and surrender to the insanity. You must recognize that retreating is not failure. Retreating is sometimes the necessary action for survival. Notice Ronny's final comments as he accepted the need to retreat so that he would finally move on with his career and take back his life:

> *All along, I felt paranoid, like it was just me. I knew I was an outsider and I kept working harder and harder to try to please Chelsea. After the name calling and the*

formal letter of reprimand in my file, I was able to accept that there was nothing I could do to remedy the situation. I even went to counseling to make sure that I wasn't really the problem. I consulted with my doctor and shared my anxiety and depression. The first time I shared my scenario, my doctor replied with a chuckle, "Looks like it is time for you to find a new job; you can't continue working under these conditions." I relied heavily on my personal friends and close allies at work to hear me out and get their advice. Every arrow pointed to a corrupt environment and a boss who would never possess the skills necessary to exemplify leadership. Once I heard the same message from multiple people (whom I greatly respected), I finally accepted that I wasn't really the problem and that it was time for me to move on. I felt like the cement shoes had been taken off. I could rise to the water line and finally breathe again.

When you realize that you have reached a point of no return, you must retreat. *Run. Flee. Escape. Retreat!* It's OK. You trying to work and live in unbearable conditions doesn't benefit the kids, and it isn't good for you or for anyone else involved. Even Ronny's own physician (who is removed from the situation) recognized the danger of remaining in such a stressful environment. You may have already reached your threshold and may be looking back and asking yourself the same questions Ronny asked himself. He questioned himself. He blamed himself. However, when he stepped back and evaluated his situation, the facts point to organizational chaos and adversarial conditions. Ronny's reflections were his wake-up call:

Wow, how did I get here? How did I become the type of person who has to whisper behind cubicles, refrain from sharing good ideas, and has to keep my head down in meetings like an abused puppy hiding in the corner? I'm here for kids, I always have been, so how did I get to the point that I was acting like a kid?

Ronny was living in fear of stepping on egos, living in fear of getting a letter in his file, simply responding with "yes" or "no" in order to get through each day, and hoping to please his boss, knowing he had no added value in her eyes. He even resorted to looking at his calendar and plotting the timing of entering a room in order to avoid any of his adversaries. Finally, Ronny reached a point of self-realization when the tiny voice inside his head whispered, *"How did I get here? This isn't me. How is this making a difference for kids?"* At that moment, a light went off for him, and his retreat will have a lasting (healthy) impact on his future.

RETREATING BEGINS WITH SHIFTING YOUR ATTITUDE

When you reach a "how did I get here?" moment because you are at the bottom of the dunk tank wearing cement shoes, you have met your personal threshold. This is the climactic moment when you experience a paradigm shift and see things more clearly than ever before. You will never look at the situation the same ever again. You have discovered the all-encompassing effects of injustice, corruption, manipulation, egos, nepotism, and greed that have consumed your career and well-being. Your experiences negatively impacted your psyche, family, and life balance. You know that there is no option other than to retreat as quickly as possible. Just like Ronny, you may need an attitude adjustment. (Don't worry, we don't mean *that* type of attitude adjustment!)

Ronny experienced his first attitudinal shift when Chelsea served him with a formal written reprimand. For the first time, he saw his circumstances for what they were. He cleared the lenses of his dunk tank goggles and saw his adversary smiling and laughing while reaching into a bucket of balls. In that moment, he accepted that he had to retreat if he wanted to save his career, integrity, and sanity. This shift in Ronny's perception and attitude was necessary to initiate long-term change for the rest of his own life.

LOOK FOR ALTERNATIVES AND OPPORTUNITIES

As you retreat, begin searching for alternatives to your current situation. You will experience grief because you are losing something prominent in your life. Your attitude will change as you realize that things will never be the same because you've made the decision to leave. Shifting your mindset to solutions and sustainability rather than survival will begin the healing process that is necessary for you, both personally and professionally. You must intentionally shift your thinking from defense to offense. Before you make a move, stop a moment and catch your breath. Give yourself time to devise a plan for exiting the tank.

Let's examine how Robert Grayson, the superintendent of schools in Vermont, from Chapter 4, looked for alternative job opportunities. If you remember, Robert had good intentions with his reading program. He wanted to support student achievement, but the emotional driving force of jealousy propelled an adversary to start throwing dunk tank balls. The community member assumed the school board member was receiving preferential treatment. After the fiasco, Robert retreated and began looking for a new job. Here's what he had to say about his experience:

I knew that there was no option for staying in my district with the entire community coming out of the woodwork. All the rumors would never be reconciled. The damage had been done and there was no rectifying my credibility. I took some time to process everything with my wife and we talked through all of our options. I also reached out to a close, personal friend. We discussed things that I could have done differently along the way, but even more importantly, my friend helped me capitalize on my interests and talents and begin the search for my next step in life. I had to support my family somehow.

My friend, Gary, whom I have known since college, helped me to focus on my talents rather than on my deficits. We began looking for alternatives without even realizing it. He reminded me that I had always wanted to teach at the university level and that the timing was never quite right in the past. He also reminded me that I wanted to travel. He knew me well enough to start pointing me towards some alternatives. Together, we listed some viable jobs on a sheet of paper that I could start applying for. There were many educational positions available that required my skillset and the ability to travel. There were also positions to teach as an online professor or online curriculum project director. Doing something different would afford me life experiences that I wouldn't otherwise have had. I was grateful to have options.

Since Robert Grayson had already experienced an attitude shift, he was able move on by searching for viable options that would be the next step in his career. Retreating allowed Robert to redirect his career in a new and exciting direction. He could effectively reinvent himself. This will be discussed more in Chapters 9 and 10, but as this topic relates to the ideals of retreating, shifting one's mindset and looking for alternatives is a saving grace no matter when it comes in relation to the timing of dunk tank trauma.

RETREAT TO LOGICALLY DEVELOP YOUR SKILLS

After you take some time to strategize your retreat and start experimenting with alternatives and opportunities, the most logical next step is to begin developing yourself for your next career move. Consider Tonya Rivera, the assistant superintendent of human resources, who fell prey to revenge during her adversarial dunk tank episode discussed in Chapter 2. The school board vice president had launched an entire arsenal of revenge-filled ammunition directly at her for firing a relative. Tonya subconsciously reached her point of no return and came up with the viable option to leave education altogether. She moved to corporate America with her human resource skills. Notice how Tonya developed her skills to prepare for her next career move:

> *My friends used to always make fun of me when I would tell them the idiotic decisions and bureaucratic red tape that prevented good decision-making in my district. They were appalled at the lack of logic and realistic interpretation of policy. Once I realized that I could be doing the very same job in the business world and could possibly escape the establishment mentality, I knew I needed to take a few steps to ensure I was marketable with skills equal to those in the business world.*
>
> *I reached out to my friends who were currently in the business sector and asked them for the key factors that hiring managers look for in new employees. After our discussions, I identified several things that I needed to develop and learn. I dedicated my last few weeks working as the*

*assistant superintendent to absorbing as much new infor-
mation as possible about current human resources practices, networking with my professional colleagues outside
of the district, and focusing on learning best practices for
leadership. I had a plan, and that plan helped sustain me
during my last few weeks in a school district.*

—*TONYA RIVERA,*
ASSISTANT SUPERINTENDENT, TEXAS

This narrative exudes a strong example of resilience. Tonya
had experienced the most detrimental effects of revenge.
Through her attitude transformation, she found an alternative
to her current job and was able to evaluate her new goals and
outcomes. She refocused her life in a positive direction.

Not only did Tonya have a plan for her own career resilience,
her positive mindset allowed her to give 100 percent while at
work each day. Even though she was the victim of revenge and
in the process of a job search, she chose not to retaliate. Quite
the contrary, she stepped up her game and continued to give her
personal best each and every day with the intent of setting up
the department for a successful transition with her replacement.

RELY ON YOUR ALLIES FOR GUIDANCE WHILE RETREATING

You may have a clear plan for moving forward with your
career and a plan for honing the skills you will need for your next
career engagement. Even with a good plan, though, you may feel
yourself regressing into anger, resentment, disappointment,
and doubt. This is normal and those feelings may take time to
dissipate. Your anxiety may be generated by the unknown and
the fear of falling into a similar scenario in your new job. Mixed

emotions and self-questioning will surface. Transforming negatively charged feelings into healthier emotions will be your saving grace.

You may want to consider visiting a counselor or connecting with friends who are well grounded and exceptional listeners. It may take "telling your story" several times over to fully move on from your dunk tank scars. You may need encouragement and hope. Reaching out to others is an essential part of healing when you are forced to retreat. If you have been blaming yourself and accepting an environment of wrongdoings, and then finally realize *you are not fault*, you must seek help to get out of the school leader's dunk tank.

Remember, this book was written because we wanted to share the stories of school leaders who might not be able to repair adversarial conditions or turn their adversaries into allies. They couldn't *fix* the situation. So they had to change their circumstances. In many cases, that meant changing careers or, at the very least, their place of employment. Many of the school leaders we interviewed told us they wish they had been prepared to deflect the dunk tank balls that were thrown at their targets with accurate aim. These school leaders wish they had exerted control and seen the red flags along the way. And when it finally became clear that they couldn't repair the damage caused by their adversaries, they wish they would have known when and how to retreat while simultaneously developing a strategy to move on to another organization. They needed help. And if you are in a similar situation, you need help, too.

Notice how Cynthia Smolinski, a former school business official, works through her mental anguish, still to this day, by reaching out to her friends and counselor:

It's like I'm a war veteran survivor who still has flashbacks of the battlefield or securing a bridge that was going to be blown up by the Viet Cong. It's been a couple of years now and I still go to counseling. God knows how much I've spent on my sessions. Some days are really, really bad and other days are bearable. Being blamed for stealing money from the petty fund accounts just broke me. It was an allegation that killed my career.

But I know that I will get through it. I know that life could be worse. I work hard each day to replace the terrible memories of my job with images of things that make me happy: my kids, summertime, daffodils. I love daffodils. I try to make sure that my kids don't see me moping around the house. I know that I will be OK. I really do know that and believe that.

I involuntarily retreated in order to not face termination proceedings. I could have fought for my job and won because I didn't steal anything. But what would that have gotten me? A bigger target on my back and more stress.

It really can be a sick business . . . education, that is. But it can also be so fulfilling too. It is such a two-faced district to be in. I know I'm better off not being there. My friends save me each and every day by helping me to laugh at those crazies who I left behind. It still hurts, but I'm working on it. That's all I can do: work on it some more.

—CYNTHIA SMOLINSKI,
FORMER BUSINESS OFFICIAL, IOWA

As we work to restructure our minds, it is helpful to understand that dunk tank experiences can either destroy you or build you into something bigger and better. Reaching out to our allies is necessary for healing to begin. Allies can also help us plan, productively and purposefully, for the future. After all, we cannot sit still forever. We were leaders to begin with; it's who we are.

WHAT HAVE YOU GAINED?

While you are purposefully planning your retreat, evaluate what you have. After the waters have subsided, what are you left with? What have you learned? How will what you now know make you a better leader?

After distilling the emotions that you may have experienced in the dunk tank, you may find that you are now able to view— and review—your life with a clearer perspective. With the emotional insights you have gained, you may discover that you are able to do the following:

- Reframe problems more constructively
- Confront any kind of self-deception when it arrives at your doorstep
- Challenge your negative belief systems
- Prepare to equip yourself with enhanced "proactive paranoia"
- Examine the big picture behind organizational structures
- Create a skill set that will help you to outwit defeat
- Assist and mentor others who need your help as an ally

You may never fully understand why you ended up in the dunk tank, but believe it or not, you were meant to experience what you went through. Perhaps you needed to learn something about yourself. Or maybe you needed to have the experience so that you could be better equipped to help others when they face similar circumstances. We believe that one of our roles is to mobilize an emotionally intelligent army of leaders who will help their colleagues learn how to tread water, plan an escape out of dunk tank scenarios, and grow from the experience. We would not be able to fulfill those roles had we not experienced the dunk tank firsthand.

In the following narrative, notice how a former high school assistant principal transformed her career into one that is focused on helping her colleagues who still work in the field of education:

I've always been a good writer and a great editor. My friends in college used to give me their research papers to look at before they handed them in. I love reading and writing. So after leaving my school because my principal was an absolute monster (he thought I was trying to take his job), I started looking for work at a few publishers because I love writing so much. I thought maybe I could become an editor or something.

Well, it just so happened that I landed a job as an assistant editor for one of the top five publishers in the nation. And just last week, I was promoted to editor for their K–12 division of children's literature. It's funny because my friends are now calling me to try to get their stuff published.

I really love what I do, and now I feel like I can overcome any obstacles that get in my way because I've been through it all (and worse) before. I'm so much more skilled at communicating, recognizing potential problems before they become big problems, and I help out people in the field of education, too. It's the best of both worlds.

Certainly, I wish I never met Bruce (my former principal), but at the same time, I'm glad I met him. I'm stronger now. And if I didn't hate working for him, I might not have searched for a job in publishing where I'm happier now.

—JENNY BAINBRIDGE,
FORMER ASSISTANT PRINCIPAL, CONNECTICUT

Jenny's story demonstrates a "What have you gained?" attitude that will take her to new levels of leadership. This brief glimpse into Jenny's experiences illustrates the power of turning off negativity and turning on emotional creativity. It is through our own meaning-making experiences (including failures and dunk tank misery) that we are able to arrive at new frontiers.

LOOKING BEHIND YOU

Good things happen to bad people and, conversely, bad things happen to good people. If you are a victim of the school leader's dunk tank, then you are fully aware of this truth. Making sense of this truth and turning it into a positive idea requires insight and careful reflection. "Everything happens for a reason" is a certitude that many people embrace for the simple reason that most people can endure difficult times if we understand it is for a greater purpose and will produce an outcome even greater than ourselves. You just have to be courageous enough to look for the *reason*.

Be willing to examine your dunk tank experience and determine if there was a positive outcome. It could be that what you learned from the negative experience will help you be successful in your new endeavor. Even if you had to retreat, you might be able to look back and see how your failed experiences actually benefitted you. Your decision to quit might be something that Polybius (whose quote opened this chapter) would commend. So go with it.

We can either move on and look back, or we can move on and not look back. Some people would argue that not looking back will help you get on with life and put the worst experiences behind you. We contend otherwise, however. Not because looking back is fun or easy, but because doing so can help you be your best going forward. Take a look at how the experience of Eric Watson, a former superintendent of schools who is now the principal of a K-5 school, differs from the personal struggles Cynthia Smolinski shared earlier:

> *I managed to escape the wrath of my board before they took aim and fired at me for good. I knew that there was no chance in hell they were going to extend my contract, so I sought refuge by looking for positions during what I knew would be my final year with the district. When the new board members took office after winning their elections, I knew I only had so much time to land on my feet. Sometimes, I look back and have so much anger for what they did to me and what they blamed me for, but I've learned to channel that into a "thank God I'm outta there" attitude that drives me to become even better than I was then—and I was a superintendent, for God's sake. I've learned that morale is such a huge thing. In a way, I dismissed staff morale—in regard to all of the new regulations coming down the pike, a new curriculum, and everything added to the teachers' plates—and maybe I wasn't sensitive enough and that came back to bite me.*

> —ERIC WATSON,
> PRINCIPAL, IOWA

We don't want to discount the pain that Cynthia still feels and is working through—especially since she did not land a new position in education and Eric did. What we contend is that looking back can offer greater insights into ourselves even during a time where self-critique seems so senseless and out of reach. Looking backwards—in order to refine solutions rather than to remember the previous pain—is a good thing.

Quitting is something that needs to be placed within our toolkit. Forget the statistics on educators' and school leaders' turnover rates and how student achievement suffers because of it. Student achievement will always suffer when adversity exists and when adult misbehavior exists. We hate to say that, but it is true. All we can do is strive to minimize the adversity and try our best to diffuse situations before they lead to our drowning.

Don't shoulder any guilt for quitting or retreating from the dunk tank just because you are going to add to the statistics of failed organizational consistency across organizational designs. It is your right to find peace when there is an unsolvable war going on around you. You owe it to yourself to prevail. In fact, you must prevail in order to reignite your passion for making a difference. You owe no one else anything.

Retreating is essential to ensuring balance and proactively addressing the small health and career issues before they become unmanageable. You must give yourself permission to retreat and to feel and own your emotions. They are yours. They are real. They belong to you. How you choose to respond to those emotions will make or break your career, but always remember: you can choose to have an out if you can recognize that someone with authority over you wants you out.

The whole purpose of education is to turn mirrors into windows.
—Sydney J. Harris

CHAPTER 9

Prevailing in Your Leadership Career

T*he business of education is sometimes a very unforgiving place. If you mess up once or cannot work through dunk tank situations, you may find yourself looking for work in another field. All of your hard work over the years can come to a screeching halt at the drop of a hat. Four years of undergraduate coursework. Two more for a master's degree. Two more for a leadership certificate. Lots more for a doctorate. Incredible amounts of preparation and investments are made, all with a vision of making a positive impact on*

our profession. Gotta pass the state certification tests, too. Incredible responsibilities in the field. High levels of stress. Many sleepless nights. Working with kids and thinking about working with kids saved me from deep depression. The love of helping them will always still be within my bones. Working with kids is easy; working with adults is hard. Working with adversarial adults is even harder, and working with irrational, blood-hungry, revengeful adults is unbearable. The profession has its ups and downs, I know that. Victories and defeats. You can be blackballed forever too. Perhaps never, ever forgiven, either.

There is no shame in being a deli manager for a frozen foods company, but that is where all of my hard work in education and my own educational preparation for doing good things for people put me. All because of a DWI. On job applications, I have to check the box that says "yes" to the question: Have you ever been convicted of a crime?

Now, I'm at the deli counter. I've worked here for three years while trying to get back into education. No one will even interview me. It's tough to sleep at night. I gotta believe that there is something more in store for me. I gotta believe that I'm gonna be OK. I gotta work hard to get back into shape. Maybe one closed door will open another one. I gotta believe that, even while I'm throwing out expired lamb shanks, something has to happen. Something good has to happen.

—CHEYENNE TATUM,
FORMER SUPERINTENDENT, ARIZONA

Cheyenne experienced the leadership dunk tank to the point that she was drawn out of the water by life guards, resuscitated back to life, and airlifted to safety. Her current reality is "deli manager," but that is not where Cheyenne's talents lie.

Cheyenne's adversaries pitted against her and the result was her own self-defeating coping measures—behaviors that spiraled out of control. After the trauma, drama, and devastation of sinking to the bottom of the tank and drowning, Cheyenne feels like she will never be the same. Her recovery will take time. The school leader's dunk tank became a life-altering event for her—a mile marker, a game changer. Her circumstances impacted her mental health, physical health, family, friends, colleagues, and her personal and professional edge. To fully recover from the adversarial tactics launched at her would require a treatment plan to not only recover from the tragic series of events, but also to rehabilitate her to the extent that she could come back even stronger.

While Cheyenne was experiencing the tactics of her adversaries, she only had the wherewithal to look into the mirror; she could only see herself and a very small area encircling the architecture of her own face. She only saw one solution. Her dunk tank recovery plan took time to develop, and consistency and objectivity to enact, but in the years following the loss of her position as a superintendent, we are happy to report that she is prevailing. Cheyenne can now look out her window and gaze as far as the eye can see, and she can of dream possibilities far beyond her line of vision. She not only prevailed, but she came back stronger. Cheyenne now owns her own business. She created a print and digital phonics program that has taken off. In her reflection below, you can see a tremendous transformation compared to the narrative that opened this chapter:

> *For me, working the deli counter was rock bottom. I decided to use this opportunity to practice leadership and develop relationships—even at the deli counter. The*

unique thing about the deli counter is you get "regulars." These regulars often dropped by after work in a rush to dart home and make a meal as they were frazzled from the happenings of their work day. I committed myself to listening and encouraging.

I'll never forget the day that Derrick Torrance commended me on my exceptional service skills and unique knack for offering small wisdoms far beyond the qualifications of working at a deli shop. Derrick started to probe into my life story and learned that I was a product of some corruption. He saw that I was someone who simply had to learn a very tough life lesson. I didn't sugarcoat my mistakes and poor decisions; I simply conveyed what I learned. I shared my new life mantra to support those around me no matter what position I was in. I would give 110 percent.

Derrick had experienced something similar in his past and now worked for an educational technology software company. He said they were hiring educational consultants and were in search for someone who "fit." Derrick's company was more interested in culture, climate, and a skillset that included emotional intelligence versus hiring those with blanket knowledge in the field of education. He sensed my emotional strength and compassion even amidst my past choices. As Derrick left the deli counter that day, he handed me his business card and said, "You are exactly what we are looking for and I think you should consider applying."

The rest is history. I didn't see the deli counter as beneath me, but rather the place I needed to be in order to start practicing the values I most believed in—those core beliefs and values that I embraced that first year in my fourth-grade classroom. I was changing myself and realigning my values. My time at the deli transcended from survival into prevailing from a very dark situation. Things happen for a reason and I will be forever grateful that I had the opportunity to work that deli counter and connect with Derrick. I am a changed woman, a happier woman, and I wouldn't be who I am today if I hadn't experienced the dunk tank. What doesn't kill us really does make us stronger. Cliché, yes, but 100 percent true.

—CHEYENNE TATUM,
FORMER SUPERINTENDENT, ARIZONA

Cheyenne didn't simply survive, she prevailed. That's what this book is about: *prevailing.* Cheyenne took initiative to turn a dark situation into an opportunity to learn and grow. She may not have drowned if she had the dunk tank survival guide and knew which safety precautions to carry out, but her experience gave her greater wisdom in her new position. Ultimately, her phonics program became integrated into the technology platform of her new employer's company.

If Cheyenne had been better equipped to handle adversarial conditions, she may never have stepped foot into the tank. At a minimum, the right insights would have prevented her from drowning. We wished that we had the appropriate strategies in our tool belt before we experienced the dunk tank ourselves. However, anyone can look back and say, "I wish I would have—" or "If I only did that." It is with our greatest failures that victories lie around the corner, but we have to look for triumph, taste it, feel it, and believe in it. In fact, one of the tenets of truly prevailing is *you've gotta want it!*

Below, you will find a series of ten helpful tips for prevailing in your career. While we focus on professional career redesign, the professional aspects of one's career are directly related to the personal aspects of one's life. After all, school leadership is more of a *lifestyle* than a job. That said, it's important to keep our work in proper perspective. The Ten Ideological Practices of Dunk Tank Survivors will help you find the right balance so that you don't end up feeling like the responsibilities of the world (or at least your district) rest on your shoulders.

THE TEN IDEOLOGICAL PRACTICES OF DUNK TANK SURVIVORS

1. STOP EXTERNAL SITUATIONS FROM POLLUTING YOUR INTERNAL STATE

If you are distressed by anything external, the pain is not due to the thing itself but to your own estimate of it; and this you have the power to revoke at any moment.
—MARCUS AURELIUS

Objectivity and rational thought are key strengths we found in educators who have strong emotional intelligence. In addition, a strong understanding of the emotional driving forces, adversarial tactics, and law of "aligned relatedness" will equip you with the toolbox you need to combat your own perceptions that are fueling your internally emotional state of mind. The first essential move you must make to correct your adversarial situation is to identify those stressors that are altering your perception. Refuse to allow your adversaries to change your self-perception and situational perception with their cunning use of the emotional driving forces of jealousy, revenge, skepticism and validity, discrimination, racism and inequality, or being held accountable. Remember, fear is a governing driving force for adversaries everywhere. You may be operating out of fear of something that hasn't even happened yet because so many tactics have already been used against you.

When trust is absent, leadership is absent. Your adversaries are very real. If you have allowed the distrust and corruption to consume you, then you must wrestle with it, objectify it, call it by its name, and put an end to your own misconceptions. Tactically, you must move from defense to offense. The first steps are to *stop* guessing what is going to happen, *stop* making assumptions about your adversaries, and *start* implementing rational strategies. Whether your adversaries hit your target or not, you will be stronger, and your state of mind will be healthy, firm, flexible, and fun.

2. USE MINDFULNESS TO PROTECT AND PRESERVE

> *On life's journey, faith is nourishment, virtuous deeds are a shelter, wisdom is the light by day, and right mindfulness is the protection by night.*
>
> **—BUDDHA**

Mindfulness is about focusing on one's thoughts, emotions, and sensations without judgement, with intent, and with full acceptance. Your dunk tank experience may have left you feeling bitter, resentful, hurt, or angry. These are your feelings. This is your current state of mind. You own them and they are neither right nor wrong. This is how you feel and nobody can change that, nor do they need to change it. Acknowledging these feelings and allowing yourself to feel the way you feel will provide you an avenue to gain control and move forward.

You must be intentional and find moments to re-center yourself—even while at work. Reflect on what has brought you joy in the past. Seek opportunities throughout the day to shift your thoughts from external stressors to viable choices. Find a balance between what fills you up and what depletes you. Close, personal friends may fill you up, while vertical relationships may deplete you—so make time to enjoy the relationships that nourish you. The point of mindfulness is to be aware of your thoughts, emotions, and surroundings. That awareness will empower you to have agency of the small things over which you have control—and let go of the things you can't control. Notice how Emily Walker, a current elementary school principal, uses the art and science of mindfulness during the day while being a principal:

> *My superintendent will come in and turn the office upside down by criticizing everything we are doing. There are too many files lying around, there is a boy sitting on the nurse's cot without supervision, the teachers are not signing out when they leave the building for lunch. You name it, he criticizes it. When he leaves, I simply go into my office for ten minutes. That's all I need. My secretary knows my routine. I close my door. I turn on my iPod, shove some earbuds in my ears, and put some Sinatra on. Then, I start coloring. Seriously. I color in these cool coloring books that I found at the supermarket. All sorts of patterns for me to trace, shade, and highlight. I use Crayola crayons like my kindergartners.*
>
> *I'm not joking! It works. It calms me down. It lowers my anxiety. I forget about Godzilla who storms into my office*

and steps on everything, including me. I'm not gonna let him get to me. I can't. I won't. I love my kiddos too much to let it eat me alive.

—EMILY WALKER,
ELEMENTARY PRINCIPAL, DELAWARE

Emily's choice to engage her senses enables her to focus on the here and now and on what's really important in her life. Coloring is just one of the many ways that mindfulness can come alive. For every colorful sketch she makes, Emily's senses absorb that color. She looks at it, appreciates it, and forgets about "Godzilla."

3. ATTACH EMOTIONAL DRIVING FORCES TO DEPERSONALIZE ATTACKS

There is a huge amount of freedom that comes to you when you take nothing personally.
—DON MIGUEL RUIZ

If anything, this book provides you with insights into some of the emotional driving forces and adversarial tactics so you can recognize the cogs, traps, and barriers that your adversaries might use to derail you. Whether you are standing on the platform or have already been pushed into the dunk tank, we encourage you to analyze your adversaries.

Ask yourself these questions: Why do my adversaries respond the way that they do? Are they covering up weakness? Are they seeking power? What is their motivating force? What drives them? Then, write down what you discover. By identifying and naming these forces and tactics, you have a better chance at deescalating the situation rather than reacting to it. Your insights will comfort you. They will.

If you see your "proactive paranoia" turning into unhealthy paranoia, stop and evaluate the situation. Create a plan of escape so that you are ready if things become unbearable. Gather empirical information. Look for patterns and habits. Figure out what provokes your adversaries as well as what positively motivates them. Try to get the facts.

Most importantly, your own ego needs to be doused. Don't let it get in the way. Although it may be impossible to change your adversaries' misconceptions, it is still important to understand how and why they operate the way that they do. What you will very likely discover is that that their behavior isn't about you. It is about them and how they perceive and react to the world. Depersonalizing their merciless attacks will empower you to respond with compassion.

4. Use Your Voice to Dissuade Confrontation

> *The two words "information"*
> *and "communication" are often*
> *used interchangeably, but they*
> *signify different things.*
> *Information is giving out;*
> *communication is getting through.*
> **—Sydney J. Harris**

Effective communication is most difficult when conflict exists. It is even harder to communicate effectively when feelings of hatred, revenge, or fear are present. Communication isn't about winning or losing; it is about navigating through the situation with as much diplomacy and accuracy as possible.

In Chapter 7, we looked at the process for non-violent communication. The four easy steps which govern non-violent communication—observations, feelings, needs, requests—will help guide you to mastering confrontation in a formulaic way until it becomes a natural and automatic way to respond. You never want to let the little things become big things. Confrontation is something that most people try to avoid at all costs—especially in a new workplace or with someone who you want to impress.

In marriages, in churches, and in friendships we all want to avoid confrontation. No one wakes up wanting to start a war, unless you are a terrorist. But non-violent, positive confrontation isn't bad. In fact, the most confident and self-assured people we've met understand how to communicate their feelings in a kind and factual way. They've learned how to address a situation without attacking the person. But we aren't saying confrontation is easy. Even though it often yields positive outcomes, we know from experience and from our own journeys in the school leader's dunk tank that confrontation (especially communicating ones' feelings) can be the most difficult response to offer. Learning the art of confrontation is probably the toughest lesson we've mastered in our own careers.

Remember: most times, your adversaries do not set out with intentional, personal, evil motives to destroy you; your injuries are simply a byproduct of their flexed power, self-preserving egos, or race to get to the top. Adversaries believe that the last (wo)man standing wins. You may be able to avoid getting run over by diplomatically addressing these ego-hungry adversaries so they become aware of the impact of their actions.

5. COUNTERACT YOUR NEGATIVE DIGITAL FOOTPRINT TO REVITALIZE YOUR NEW IMAGE

Don't necessarily avoid sharp edges.
Occasionally, they are
necessary for leadership.
—DONALD RUMSFELD

Politics are politics, I get that. Really. You can't remove yourself from politics when the business is politics. But smearing someone is another thing. With the work I do advocating for multiple groups of professionals, sometimes money and emotions get in the way of people doing the right thing. I worked on so many projects with so many different teams. I knew that others would oppose my viewpoints, and that is okay—opposition is the essence of arriving at consensus which provides ways for us to question our leaders who are supposed to be accountable to the voters and tax payers. But smearing my reputation with hateful blogs, mistruths, and cowardly insults led me to want to look into how to get some of this nonsense to stop.

Pictures of me, my family, cartoons of me, hateful posts, allegations of money laundering (which are false), and so many other terrible things that were posted on the Internet definitely led to me not getting a new contract from the board. I'm most certain of that. You give someone something to believe in and they will always question you before they question the validity of the Internet. People think the Internet is 100 percent scripture. The sad thing is that no one will ever uncover blog or website administrators who bashed me because it is an invasion of their privacy. Yet I'm the one who gets victimized. It really is a terrible thing. So sad. We teach our students how to respect the Internet and use it properly, for good. Yet, revengeful adults use it to attack and they are protected with the right to attack.

—OWEN PYZIK,
FORMER SUPERINTENDENT OF SCHOOLS, TENNESSEE

We now live in a world of live-stream videos, SnapChat, Facebook, Twitter, Instagram, Amazon reviews, and LinkedIn. We receive social information within a nanosecond of its inception. For all its benefits, the Internet's ability to spread information quickly can be a challenge for school leaders—particularly with adversaries who create false or damaging digital footprints for their victims. Social media can be a positive leveraging tool as much as it can be a career-crippling nuclear catastrophe. Cyber-bullying, misinformation, misperceptions, misinterpretations, slander, and compromised privacy are all very real. This new digital frontier requires us to monitor social platforms on a regular basis to stay ahead of rumors, needs, and circumstances. It also requires us to weigh each and every word we share, post, or Tweet very carefully—because there are no takebacks online.

Your digital footprint (whether created by you or by someone else's posts *about* you) will last much longer than most of the other adversarial conditions you endure. Like Owen, whose adversaries posted blogs and comments to spread false allegations about him laundering money (a crime he never committed), if you end up in the dunk tank , you may have tabloid-like news articles posted about you. Owen has left this toxic environment, but his digital footprint, tainted by adversarial blogs with nasty postings, continues to follow him. When a potential employer searches his name, those articles could very well prevent him from securing a new job.

To counteract this social phenomenon, you must be intentional while online. You may have to work even harder than your nemesis to outnumber the negative digital hits with the good ones. For example, an author (who asked to remain anonymous) encountered continuing dunk tank throws from her adversaries even after being gone from her school district for a year. Her adversaries attacked her books, which are reviewed and listed on Amazon.

She had written a book in a genre outside of education, but as a result of her adversarial situation in her school district, an adversary posted a book review bashing her character as a person. The comment didn't directly address the text, but denounced her credibility as a writer. All the other reviews listed were verified purchases with four or five star ratings and eloquent, positive comments by highly credible people who even hold doctorates. The negative comment stuck out like a sore thumb. Nonetheless it reduced the customer review satisfaction percentage. She ended up being strategic and asking her close family and friends and ally groups to write reviews to follow the negative one so that it counteracted and minimized the negative review that finally became sandwiched in between the positive reviews. The adversary's comment wasn't a reflection of the book, it was a cunning move filled with jealousy and revenge.

Like this author, you may have to work strategically to clean up the tracks left behind. To counteract a negative digital footprint, use the power of search engine optimization by doing the following things:

1. Join and comment on social media posts, news article posts, and professional journals. Share your hope, your lessons learned, words of encouragement, or your expertise. Support others by giving positive feedback.

2. Start a blog to provide regular positive articles and educational learnings. This will populate in search engines when your name is searched. You want your name search to pull up the most recent and active entries.

3. Create new domains and build a website with strong educational content. Place backlinks to your own personal website to show your knowledge base and current learnings. Showcase what you know and what you are good at.

4. Purchase a domain name that consists of your name. It will rise to the top of the Google search engine.

5. If you made mistakes in your past, don't make them again, of course, but write about them on blogs, etc. if you are able to. Confront your past mistakes, but help others through their problems or issues and use your new wisdom as a tool to help them.

6. EQUALIZE YOUR CALENDAR TO CREATE BALANCE

Balance is not something you find;
it's something you create.
—JANA KINGSFORD

Creating balance is pretty simple math. Make sure that the time you spend doing what you enjoy is equal to the time you spend doing what you must (even if you don't necessarily enjoy what you must do). Do things and activities that nourish you, especially if you start to feel unhappy or unduly stressed or tired. Balance will not just happen by making a declaration that you want a balanced life. It requires action. Physically and literally, look at your calendar and balance it before work, during (small breaks), and after to ensure that you are socially and emotionally nourishing yourself at a rate equal to or greater than the rate at which you are being depleted. Schedule activities that give you pleasure—you know, things that you are good at or make you feel good about yourself (music, exercise, art, volunteering for a non-profit, reading, shopping, cooking, etc.). Build these activities into habits.

7. Establish a Confidant for Accountability

F-E-A-R has two meanings:
"Forget Everything and Run," or
"Face Everything and Rise."
The choice is yours.
—Zig Ziglar

In moments of contentment, peace, and centeredness, it is much easier to use diplomacy and remove emotions than to give the benefit of the doubt to others. But as the heat turns up, with appointments being double booked, multiple trainings taking place, parent complaints, deadlines, fire drills, and legal issues piling up all around you, it is much more difficult to maintain balance and indifference to adversarial situations.

It is vital to make one of your personal allies a confidant with whom you are committed to routinely touching base. In good times, bad times, or any time, you will also need to be an accountability partner for them. Your conversations should be filled with difficult questions and honest answers. These must

CHAPTER 9· PREVAILING IN YOUR LEADERSHIP CAREER

be solution-based conversations rather than complaint festivals (even though we recognize that venting is a human need). The conversation should not take place simply for the sake of complaining; rather, it should focus on how you can take control of your response and positively impact a situation. Celebrate success and strategize challenges. Discuss these challenges and how to rise above the status of the current situation. And remember: while we strongly urge gathering allies in Chapter 8, it is what you do with those allies that will be both constructive and powerful for your future decision-making.

8. Schedule Routine Dunk Tank Check-Ups to Prevent Entropy

It's not who you are that holds you back,
it's who you think you aren't.
—Unknown

You will have moments when the tiny voice inside your head tells you something isn't quite right. Listen to it. That's your proactive paranoia at work, and it just may help you interpret warning signs and others' behaviors before it's too late. Sometimes, that voice will randomly speak up and stop you dead in your tracks. But sometimes it whispers. That's why we believe it is valuable to schedule time for intentional, scripted reflection. In other words, be proactively paranoid about *you*!

During this reflection time, revisit the tactics, principles, and strategies that support a healthy, balanced life. Ask yourself the hard questions: Am I doing my personal best? Have I dunked anyone myself? Have I interacted professionally and objectively with my adversaries? Have I allowed anyone to alter my beliefs or actions? Have I compromised my personal ethical code? Am I making an impact on others? Is it time to plan an exit strategy? Can I continue in this organization knowing that corruption will continue? These types of reflections are socially and emotionally formative for the educator within you. Just as we offer our students formative assessment tools to check in on what we know, need to know, or don't know, we as adults also need formative analysis time.

9. Never Waver from What's Right

The slogan "Press On" has solved and always will solve the problems of the human race.
—CALVIN COOLIDGE

Even when the ball hits the target and you know it is time to flee, this is not the time to waver. This is the time to stand tall, maintain excellence, set the organization up for success, and give your adversaries and the organization everything they have asked of you as you exit with grace. Good things happen to bad people and, likewise, bad things happen to good people. Just because you have found yourself in turmoil doesn't give you the liberty to show weakness or reduce yourself to similar, petty, or hurtful behaviors. You must hold your head high and pretend that you are happy and confident even though you feel crippled inside. Be thoughtful, be kind, be considerate, serve others, and make an impact even as you exit the tank while dodging balls being thrown at the back of your head. Do not waver and do not let adversarial tactics outweigh integrity and humane professionalism.

We know it can be difficult to not take short cuts, to not let your adversaries turn you into something you are not, or to stand tall and make the correct decisions all the time. Some of the best leaders can crumble and impede their own transformation. In Chapter 6, we presented the dangers that exist when professionals rely on alcohol or pills to cope with daily pain. In the stories we shared, bad decisions were made, backbones weakened, and adversarial support grew when life became skewed for the leaders who shared their stories. But do you know what? They realized and took responsibility for their mistakes, got help, and then they helped others. When you fall, choose not to stay down. Choose to get up, press on, and do what's right.

10. FORGIVE YOURSELF AND YOUR ADVERSARIES

Anger ventilated often hurries towards forgiveness; anger concealed often hardens into revenge.
—EDWARD G. BULWER-LYTTON

The only way to release resentment is through forgiveness. If you choose not to forgive, you risk joining the adversarial club. Cheyenne's treatment plan required her to not only forgive her adversaries, but to also forgive herself for her own mistakes that culminated with her DWI. That wasn't who she was; it wasn't who she wanted to be—but it was who she had *become*. Rest assured, we understand that healing and forgiveness take time. We know it is not easy. We know that some of your memories will haunt you. But without forgiveness, there can be no true hope of a full recovery. Prevailing requires forgiving yourself and others.

We have listed Ten Ideological Practices of Dunk Tank Survivors, but you may have additional ideas or strategies to add to this list. However you choose to prepare, protect, and prevail, the actions you take and the mindset and attitude you choose are yours alone. Nobody can undo your practices. You own them; they are part of your character and how you operate inside or outside the dunk tank. When you stay focused and use these practices to strengthen yourself emotionally, mentally, and physically, you won't just survive—you will thrive.

You are a difference-maker even if you are currently at the deli counter. Remember who you are. That deli counter is only temporary until you learn what you need to learn and are equipped and renewed enough to thrive. Prevailing is not a linear concept. It is a mindset that allows you to grow—forever changing, always being flexible, and sometimes getting adventurous. Your students, colleagues, teachers, and supervisors are all depending on you. *You* need to depend on *you*, as well. You don't have to drown in the dunk tank.

EXPECT AN AFTERMATH

Even after it seems like the waters have subsided, a tsunami may follow once you have exited the dunk tank. In addition to the Ten Tenets of Truth and the Ten Ideological Practices that embrace a mindset of prevailing, we wanted to interject a final thought for you to consider after you have escaped the dunk tank. The pains may linger and random dunk tank balls may periodically blindside you. Expect it. Expect that your adversaries will continue. Below are a few adversarial actions for which you will want to be on the lookout so they don't drag you back to the water:

- An attacking e-mail out of nowhere, months or even years down the road, filled with hatred and venting remarks

- Condescending remarks made about you by an adversary to someone at your new place of employment

- Comments on blogs or articles made to try to discredit you

- Social media slander and degrading comments, posts, and even subtle undertones targeted at you

- Lost friendships and ruined professional relationships due to lies told by your adversaries

Adversaries who are filled with hatred may become even bolder in retaliation and confrontation once you are no longer employed in your dunk tank. They do not want to see you prevail, and they will try to take you down one last time if they see you move on and succeed. It may become their personal vendetta to try to see you fail long-term. They clearly have forgotten that we are in the business of making a difference in kids' lives.

Prevailing requires the Ten Ideological Practices and a keen awareness of the aftermath behaviors your adversaries may exhibit. Getting tossed into the dunk tank hurts, and it can make you question your self-worth. But if you know what is coming, you can be intentional about focusing on your talents, maintaining your personal character, and confiding in someone who can throw you a lifesaver and encourage you in the midst of challenge.

Don't let your adversaries get under your skin; that is what they want. Depersonalize their attacks, strategize your response, and move on if/when it's time. Take a moment to acknowledge your feelings, realizing that it's OK to feel hurt. But don't let them steal your sparkle. Your passion, liveliness, and leadership are working parts and pieces in the greater machine of working for kids.

There are two kinds of cherry pickers: those who choose to throw out the good cherries and wallow in all the rotten ones, and those who choose to throw out all the rotten ones and savor all the good ones.

CHAPTER 10

THRIVING ONCE AGAIN

I'm happier now. I know what matters most in my life. They say that time passes by so quickly and if you don't take a moment to stop and smell the roses, it will be too late. I couldn't have retired from being a principal, anyway, even if it was only ten more years. The stress was killing me. Don't get me wrong. I loved *my students; they are the reason I went into education in the first place. The kids were easy. It was the adults that were hard. My superintendent was nuts. She hated me from day one, and I don't know why. I was a good leader. Just not her cup of tea, I guess. I'll never really know why she did what she did to get me to leave. She was a sniper, though, my No. 1 adversary—and she was my boss! I thought she'd be on my side to support me and do what was best for kids. I guess I was wrong. Her friend took my job when I left. Hiring committees and union input.*

Give me a break. She ended up hiring her friend anyway. How could you not be a finalist when the superintendent asks for four finalists? They only interviewed six people. At the time, I was devastated and took everything personally. In retrospect, I'm stronger, more balanced, more committed, and happier. What my superintendent did was wrong, but I forgave, moved on, and focused on what really matters. I am in the difference-making business. Students and our future matter more than a superintendent's poor leadership or my negative experience.

—SYLVIA ALVAREZ-MCKENZIE,
FORMER PRINCIPAL, NEBRASKA

Think back to your first job in education. Most likely the first position you held in education was in the classroom. Remember the scent of new crayons, erasers, and glue? You put hours of thought into designing lessons and inspiring and motivating kids. You created trendy bulletin boards. You stayed up late prepping artwork or grading papers. You may have had a few restless nights during the weeks leading up to the first day of school. Your first year of teaching was a climactic moment of excitement and passion because you had just invested the past four years of school in order to experience this professional milestone:

making a difference with kids. Laughter, clapping, cheers of accomplishment, and high-fives were daily nourishments for your educator's soul. Your motives were pure, and interacting with your students brought about a huge sense of accomplishment and joy.

For Sylvia, time passed by very quickly between her first year of teaching and finding herself at the bottom of the dunk tank. And unfortunately, all the little things that were so special and meant so much got trampled by negative dunk tank experiences.

Moments of adversity force us to slow down and live in the present. In Sylvia's circumstance, she was an inherited commodity. Her superintendent didn't hire her; she was merely a preexisting employee to her boss. We are all at greater risk to enter the dunk tank when a new leader plugs into any organization. In Sylvia's case, her superintendent, who had been there just over a year, was never even willing to embrace her talents or assume positive intentions because Sylvia was never her own hiring choice. The honeymoon period was over before it began, and Sylvia never even realized that her superintendent secretly hoarded dunk tank balls all year long, waiting for the right time to start throwing pitches.

Strong leaders know that the first year of entering a new organization is all about going with the flow and creating relationships. During the second year, leaders often begin making changes, and year three often dictates radical changes if the organization warrants it. Oftentimes, leaders who enter an environment without any known allies will use their emotional driving forces to "clean house" and surround themselves with vertical and horizontal allies. They may capitalize on nepotistic personnel decisions or they may simply stand alone and act like vulnerable martyrs.

"Cleaning house" is a goal of several adversarial tactics that are implemented to self-preserve bad behavior and mask poor leadership. The upheaval may not have anything to do with their targets personally. Regardless, these "inadvertent adversarial tactics" do as much damage as "purposeful adversarial tactics." We are sure that Sylvia's experiences felt personal to Sylvia, but they really weren't. Whether you have been in the dunk tank seat yet or not, you most likely understand that finding your own happiness amidst adversity takes intentional work. You have to choose to throw away the "rotten cherries" and savor the good ones.

Dunk tank graduates understand that adversarial working conditions are temporary. They are temporary because you will either dissuade your adversaries from negative behaviors, or you will choose to exit gracefully if your repair tactics fail. The most successful dunk tank graduates resolve to learn from their mistakes and to allow challenges to make them even better leaders. Stronger. Wiser. Kinder. Less ego-driven. Understanding. Compassionate. These survivors have a new level of preparedness that will move them forward with future successes even if they have to rebuild their careers from behind the deli counter.

This chapter is a celebration of you. We are cheering you on with the full regalia of pom-poms, amplifiers, dance music, matching hair ribbons, and cheers as obnoxious and loud as a high-school pep rally. The fact that you are reading this book shows that you care, that you have the ability to reflect, and that you have a desire to positively impact the unique culture of education.

It also indicates that you are a leader who is willing to contribute to changing the politics of education. There is power in numbers, and our goal as the authors of *Escaping the School*

Leader's Dunk Tank is to rally our allies, call out the elephants, and strategize to make our own profession better—because we, too, are difference-makers.

Every child, worldwide, deserves access to inspiring educators, passionate classrooms, and collaborative stakeholders. We must refocus, join forces, and stand up to the bullies in education who are creating adversarial situations. Our kids deserve the best we have to give.

We know that you have the ability to leverage your talents, your experiences, and your leadership skills in order to overcome any adversarial tactic thrown your way. We know that you will navigate the dunk tank with grace because you understand and love this great profession. You believe in leadership. You embrace relationships. You exhibit tolerance. You sacrifice your time, wearily, day in and day out (way before 9:00 a.m. and way past 5:00 p.m.) with every fiber of your existence. You choose to communicate effectively. You embrace academic data (and research) as your foundation for decision-making within the domains of teaching, learning, and assessment. You choose to learn and grow each and every day. You choose to network and embrace the talents of others. You choose to lead by example instead of making examples of others. You inspire. You dream. And you are willing to do anything in order to make a difference with kids.

The irony is that you may have entered the dunk tank *because* you have such a high commitment to the expectations in your district, a strong work ethic, and the passion to move mountains. Somewhere along the way, you were lured into the tank by the persuasion of your adversaries in some sort of perfect storm. Your heart was in the right place and your soul and mind followed suit.

What matters now is that you not only prevail, but you feel alive and thrive again in your career. We want you to be excited each and every day when you drive to work. We want you to feel renewed and empowered when you reflect on your good work. We want you to have a peaceful outlook, knowing that your work is not just a career, it is the life flowing through your veins, and it matters. *You* matter.

As we near the end of the book we would like to share eight simple tasks that are well within your locus of control. You have the power of choice to implement and carry out these cheerleading features, no matter your present conditions and no matter what any adversaries throw your way.

When things are going great and when things are challenging, you still have the power to spot, troubleshoot, and recognize adversarial conditions. Whether you are in the dunk tank, have been in the dunk tank, or still haven't experienced the dunk tank, these tasks will launch you forward in creating positive relationships and preserving your own self-worth and purpose as a leader in education. Stay mindful of the following eight tasks and make the choice to triumph over tragedy.

EIGHT TASKS TO OPTIMIZE TRIUMPH OVER TRAGEDY

1. List Your Gratitudes

On a particularly difficult day at work, my colleague and I had experienced an inordinately high level of anxiety and stress due to the climate and corruption. Mostly we were used to it, but every now and then it got the best of one of us. On that day, the insanity made its way into my brainstem, blocking my brain pathways from reality. The stress was altering my perception to the point of nearly inducing a panic attack. Everything in our department was always due last minute; we were working our tails off while the "favorites" got long lunch breaks and went home early. The inequity, nepotism, and injustice fueled my anxiety.

I will never forget the conversation I had with Renee that day because it altered my perception and encouraged me. As I was leaving the office, my colleague said to me, "You know, as horrible as our day is going, this is still just a first-world problem. We don't have to worry about shelter, disease, famine or if our family is going to make it to a refugee camp. Our biggest challenge today is dealing with a selfish boss who happens to be getting away with murder in a corrupt organization. So although this stinks for us, we are still extraordinarily blessed."

Her comments stopped me dead in my tracks as I began reflecting on the things in my life that really mattered— the things that I was grateful for that day. Renee helped me focus on gratitude when I was in the thick of things. She had the wisdom and insight to know just what I needed to hear considering my current state of mind. I was grateful that I had Renee as a vertical ally who truly understood what I went through day in and day out behind the district curtain. Today I believe, more than ever, that a mindset of gratitude can improve my perception, no matter how horrible the day is going.

—BRENDON PALMER,
PURCHASING COORDINATOR, ALASKA

Gratitude is a mindful act that transcends corruption. It is a life preserver. Dunk tank experiences are clearly first-world problems that you can navigate through with gratefulness. Some of our biggest adversaries can be out-played by the simple act of being grateful, showing gratitude, and expressing that gratefulness to others. Gratitude requires *centering* yourself by not *comparing* yourself to anyone else. Brendon was able to realize that even though there were "favorites" in his department, and he had to double up on their work in a corrupt environment, it was still his obligation to rise far above the pettiness with gratitude. He needed to be grateful that he had a job, a car to drive, food to eat, and good health to enjoy. Had he continued to compare his situation to the perks his corrupt adversaries enjoyed, he would have sunk deeper into the tank. By reframing his mindset from victim to a governor who controls his own gratitude and removing the obstacle of comparison, Brendon was able to work with a positive attitude.

Gratitude places you in the present and shouldn't be clouded with things that have happened in the past. *What am I grateful for today?* This is the question you need to write in bold marker on a bright sticky note in plain sight of your desk, cubicle, or office. On your best day and your worst day, you should be answering this question to reel your mindset into the present and anchor yourself back to your core beliefs. Follow through and make a list of things for which you are grateful *today.* What are you grateful for right now?

2. RECOGNIZE YOUR TALENTS

We decided to ask several educators the question, "What are your educational talents?" Listen to the dialogue between Cedrick Hall, an instructional coach in South Dakota, and us (Rick/Rebecca).

R&R: Cedrick, what are your educational talents?

Cedrick: I don't have my Ph.D. like many of my friends and colleagues. I have never been an administrator, I've never had anything published or anything like that, but I work hard and love people. I know that I implement all the district initiatives. I am a Google-certified teacher, I was recognized as a district "champion," I'm working on a second master's degree in educational leadership, and I typically get high marks on my evaluations. I have strong relationships with my teachers and feel that I am very effective at facilitating professional development and supporting teachers in the classroom.

R&R: *You have listed some great achievements and recognitions that are highly notable. We want you to shift your thinking a little differently for a minute. Reflect on the past five years and tell us about your involvement and contributions to your teachers and students, school, or district. What have you contributed (no matter how big or how small) that you believe made a difference?*

Cedrick: *Oh gosh, there are so many great things that we have accomplished together at our school. We were a host school for the district technology tour and I was able to plan and support my talented teachers and students to showcase their rooms with leaders across the state. I really took the lead in our professional learning communities (PLCs) school-wide, and I strategically taught them how to create formative assessments, review student work, and plan effectively for lessons based on their data. I even supported another school, before and after school, because they wanted to use the same protocol for PLCs that we were using. I helped design weekly formative assessments aligned to our standards and it really gave us the information that we needed to differentiate for our kids and customize our reteach and enrichment time. I made brochures to go home to parents for each grade level in reading and math that listed the goals and outcomes of learning for each quarter. To increase our community* *culture and climate, I encouraged teachers to send home positive postcards. I modeled how to set up and use Class Dojo so that our parents could check student progress on their apps. I also taught many teachers how to create and navigate teacher websites. This made an overall impact on our school as we saw a rise in our parent participation and parent turnout for curriculum nights and conferences. I helped bridge the gap between home and school. These things really made a difference. Our school submitted an application for the Blue Ribbon School award, which was an in-depth process. My principal asked if I would be a lead writer and support the team by going through the application step-by-step and analyze the rubrics to make sure we didn't leave anything out. We never worked so hard, but our collaboration and teamwork paid off because we did receive the national award. We were all proud.*

R&R: It is impressive how much you have contributed to education. Thank you for your contribution to making a difference in education. We need more people like you who are talented and focused on making contributions rather than just seeking achievements. Keep up the great work that you are doing.

By shifting the question to focus on *contributions* rather than *achievements*, Cedrick could go on and on. In order to fully recognize your talents, you must think about what you *contribute*. You can see from our dialogue that Cedrick began the conversation a little uneasy, as he was very modest when listing his accomplishments and even focused on what he *hadn't* accomplished. After probing further with the targeted question about his contributions, he lit up as he shared all those things that he had contributed as an educational influencer—things that he never fully took credit for as he referred to "we." His interactions and contributions made a big difference in the lives of the kids, teachers, and parents of his school community. Contributions signify *community* progress and victory. Accomplishments signify being spoiled, isolated, and self-absorbed in gaining something else. They are gold stars on charts that no one is really tracking. We know you are in your career as a school leader because you want to cultivate the successes of *others*.

There is also a tendency in education to *compete* and *compare* achievements rather than celebrating the contributions. What you do to *contribute* to the greater good of your organization has a far greater impact than your personal achievements or accomplishments.

An activity that will empower you in challenging times is recognizing your own talents. Create a list of your achievements, contributions, and talents. Use these contributions, achievements, and talents to plan for new and upcoming contributions. Keep up the momentum by contributing to and influencing the minds of your students. Recognize your talents and then go on and use them!

3. CREATE AND USE AFFIRMATIONS

It's the repetition of affirmations that leads to belief. And once that belief becomes a deep conviction, things begin to happen.
—CLAUDE M. BRISTOL

Significant new research regarding the use of affirmations on both a personal and professional level reveals their power to recharge and reprogram your mind from *destruction* to *construction*. Consider the story of Janet Berkmeyer, a current assistant superintendent of curriculum and instruction in Texas:

> *When I present the data from the annual assessments, I see my school board members looking at me with daggers in their eyes. Even though they do not utter a word, it's as if they're saying "See, she didn't reach our goals this year. We missed the mark, again. We need a new assistant superintendent. She is useless. She is unskilled to lead the principals." So I make a decision: I can choose to care what they think about my leadership, or I can think about what I know about my leadership: that I'm kind, smart, purposeful, productive, and intentional with the growth plan that we have set forth. Improvement will take place. It just takes time. I keep filling my own head with what I know will happen. I must keep up the hard work of making it happen even though my supervisor and school board members think ill of me.*

While affirmations can include personalized affirmation of the "self" (e.g., I am a good person. I am a good leader. I love kids. I love myself.), the general positive alignment of transforming your thoughts (e.g., I will be OK. I will try harder at working with that person. I will treat her with kindness.) helps to affirm what you should be thinking about instead of what you are *coaxed* into thinking about. If we spend too much time on the negative, we will ultimately become negative.

As described in the narrative above, Janet's personal affirmations help create a positive mind shift that impacts her day. Janet chooses to use positive affirmations to strengthen her work day, career, and survival in the career of education.

4. ALLOW YOURSELF TO BE VULNERABLE AGAIN

This sounds like you are playing a mind game on yourself, but it really isn't meant to be perceived that way. In Brené Brown's book, *Rising Strong,* she encourages readers to embrace the concept of vulnerability: "Vulnerability is not winning or losing; it's having the courage to show up and be seen when we have no control over the outcome. Vulnerability is not weakness; it's our greatest measure of courage" (p. 5).

We must get out of the cheap seats and venture out onto the field. We must be involved and not become watchers or standby souls of the cruelty of the school leader's dunk tank. Brené Brown's ten rules of engagement for making vulnerability an ally applies to the dunk tank:

1. If we are brave enough often enough, we will fall; this is the physics of vulnerability.

2. Once we fall in the service of being brave, we can never go back.

3. The journey belongs to no one but you; however, no one successfully goes it alone.

4. We're wired for story.

5. Creativity embeds knowledge so that it can become practice. We move what we're learning from our heads to our hearts through our hands.

6. Rising strong is the same process whether you're navigating personal or professional struggles.

7. Comparative suffering is a function of fear and scarcity.

8. You can't engineer an emotional, vulnerable, and coura-geous process into an easy, one-size-fits-all formula.

9. Courage is contagious.

10. Rising strong is a spiritual practice.

Strength, courage, and vulnerability are your allies. Assume positive intentions again by recognizing how vulnerability is your friend. Become a risk-taker, knowing that it is inevitable that you will fail again. You may have made plans to exit the dunk tank and enter another career altogether. You must be brave enough to be vulnerable again. The biggest difference between your dunk tank experiences in the past and now is that you are a *dunk tank graduate* and you have the knowledge and skills to recognize the signs of future adversaries. Learn to trust again and keep vulnerability in your back pocket. You got it. Go for it!

5. Strategize Your Game Plan

You have control over strategy. There are several ways you can gain the mental upper hand through *strategy*. You must take time to map out your own professional boundaries. What are you willing to compromise and where do you draw the line? Are you willing to allow rumors about you to fly? Are you will-ing to listen to colleagues bash others behind their backs? Are you willing to party and cross the professional line to a more personal line? Are you willing to do double the work and watch your favored colleague do minimal work? Where do you draw the line? Will you use the non-violent communication strategy to confront these issues when a boundary is crossed? You must have an intentional plan to navigate the cogs and traps that your adversaries will place you in.

Notice how Regina Brown, an assistant superintendent for human resources in Florida, creates a strategy to counteract her superintendent's dunk tank:

> *We knew we had to make some cuts to staffing. We were thinking of reducing a total of 2.0 clerical full-time employees across the district . . . a .5 clerical position at four schools. This was one of fifty cuts that we needed to carry out in order to make payroll the following year and not have a deficit of $1.3 million dollars while honoring step agreements from the last contract that was going to expire in six months. My superintendent was sick of the clerical union holding tight on their desire to have a 3, 5, and 6 percent increase in salaries over the next three years of a new contract, so he came into my office and told me to put together a layoff list. Rather than just pull the trigger on so many people, I looked at things and realized that the union and I should first look at the seniority list together and have a 1:1 discussion about where budget cuts might come from. When we did this, we noticed some errors on the seniority list, so we fixed that up first. I wasn't insubordinate to my superintendent; rather, I thought through the process and realized where things needed to start.*

Here, Regina reflects on the power of strategy, both in terms of carrying out her work duties and in thinking about how to dodge dunk tank set ups by her superintendent who hated her. Regina smartly set up a process that started at the beginning with analysis *before* drastic action.

You will need to come up with a Plan A, B, and C when you are presented with adversarial conditions. Take a breath. Take a step back. Think. Mold. Strategize a plan. Don't be quick to respond. It's like the show *Survivor*. You must outwit, outplay, and outlast your opponent while also being aware of the potential damage your actions or decisions could have on you and the organization.

6. Redefine Yourself

Renewal and regeneration is the fun part of exiting the dunk tank. You have been given a fresh start to decide who you are, what you are made of, and how you will help others moving forward. You will be able to redefine yourself through personality quizzes, setting new goals, and gaining new knowledge.

You have most likely taken a variety of personality quizzes. Now is the time to wipe the slate clean and consider taking personality quizzes to better understand who you are *now*. The new you possesses greater strengths than ever before.

In addition to discovering who you are, consider what you want. Goal-setting will help you chart a new course. Write new goals in all facets of life: social goals, relationship goals, learning goals, and career goals. Post your goals and revisit them daily. Reflect, revise, and repeat. Personal growth is a never-ending cycle of renewal and recreation.

Our own experiences taught us a lot about how to prevail, but we've also learned a great deal from the good work of many authors and experts who are in our corner. Connect with external professional colleagues with the intent of learning and growing in knowledge. Read articles and blogs about leadership. Stay current, feed yourself with books (yes, David Burgess Consulting, Inc. books will get you started), renew your methodologies, discern which practices are truly the best, and build your leadership toolkit. Knowledge is a very powerful weapon against adversaries.

7. DEVELOP YOURSELF INTO A BEHIND-THE-SCENES EXPERT

I swear they had reorganized the district hierarchy chart a million times this year. Okay, that was a gross exaggeration (it was really only three), but revising a district organizational chart three times in one year is a lot of change. Titles, chain of command, reporting supervisors were all in disarray. It was the last month of school and the grand message was delivered to me by my supervisor: "Surprise, we are reorganizing the district chart again, and this time we are eliminating your position to create different positions, so you will need to interview if you would like, otherwise we do have classroom position available."

If this wasn't a dunk tank red flag, I don't know what else would be. My supervisor, Anna Lynn, was an insecure know-it-all who reacted and responded with the yip of a Chihuahua. Annoying and ego hungry, she managed people by barking orders.

After talking with several close friends, I decided to apply for the newly created director position which was the next step above my coordinator position. I knew I had the skillset and was overqualified, but Anna Lynn would never have believed this in a million years because everything was always about her micromanaging and flexing power and control. I knew it could be career suicide to interview, and if I didn't get the job, it would be the end of the road for me. But I had to try because I was qualified and had equivalent experience in my prior district, in fact. Anna Lynn was so confident that I wouldn't even pass the interview that she had two other directors from completely different departments sit in on the interview, most likely as an intimidation technique, in order to justify not hiring me.

To this day, I smile ear to ear remembering what transpired in that interview. As the technical questions were thrown my way, I rattled off research, experiences, techniques, and a strong leadership presence. The other two directors were so blown away that they said I nailed the interview and was even overqualified for the position. They were so proud of my professionalism and expertise that they wanted me for the position. The plan backfired on my boss, and I landed the job because I was an expert in my field. She was so busy controlling everyone and micromanaging and putting us in our place that she never even took the time to really get to know me and my expertise.

—Kevin Cunningham,
21st Century Coordinator, Washington

Learning, practicing, plugging in, reading, collaborating, watching, listening, and growing are all transformative dunk tank actions. Knowledge is power. Experience is power. Expertise is power. Honing your craft and practicing your skills will transform your world into a confident world of school leadership.

Kevin had been navigating the dunk tank all along. He was capable of more, but Anna Lynn never allowed him to be anything more. And that was okay, in this example, because it wasn't his place to put on a demonstration of his expertise. Behind the scenes, Kevin was dedicated to learning from others, collaborating, and going back and researching to better serve the colleagues he supported. He networked with all five of his ally groups in pursuit of becoming an expert. Kevin's experiences were real, and he sharpened his skillset to forge positive relationships. And when the timing was right, his behind-the-scenes expertise empowered him to land the next position in his career.

Becoming a behind-the-scenes expert will help you to rise above the madness and prepare for tomorrow.

8. EMPOWER OTHERS: CULTIVATE A THINK-TANK FOR YOUR COLLEAGUES

Mentoring new school leaders or someone who has the potential to be a school leader rejuvenates you. What you learn as you train and mentor others will stay with you forever.

If you recognize that a school leader is in trouble, take them under your wing and mentor them to the very best of your abilities. For that matter, your mentees don't have to be "in trouble"—find someone to mentor, because one thing is certain: trouble will come. Your care and direction may help someone get out of or, better yet, avoid the dunk tank altogether.

Jackie Bernstein, a seventeen-year veteran principal, took mentoring to heart by setting up an informal support group for her colleagues:

> When they [the new principals, assistant principals, deans, etc.] are hired, I immediately step in and make them an ally. I like to think that I'm the friendliest principal in Ohio (although the jury is still out on that!). We need to stick together. My district has a politically charged, historical legacy that is like no other. A political terrain that can be exhaustive and crippling at times.
>
> I set up monthly support group meetings that we [the administrators] all attend. It doesn't matter if you are in your first year or fiftieth year. We have to share what is going on because politics and adversity in one pocket of the district can impact an entire district. It can grow and spread like cancer. We have to look at the entire system. We have to look at what is going on everywhere if we are going to survive and thrive together.

Jackie exudes a strong systems-thinking approach to dealing with the known politics of her district. She understands the politics, how pockets create epidemics, and how we all can learn from even one experience taking place miles away even if it doesn't seem like it fits into our own leadership context.

We have a duty to serve our profession, and that duty extends well above and beyond the localized walls of education. As dunk tank survivors increase, political negligence and chaos will decrease. Sure, politics in education will always exist; we know that. But the preparation of school leaders everywhere cannot rely on coursework taught at the university level. As leaders, we must be supplementing university training and be intentional about growing and helping others to thrive. From support groups to book study groups to speaking engagements to summertime retreats, there are a myriad of ways that you can mentor your colleagues and give back to your profession.

CONTINUING THE CONVERSATION

ALTHOUGH THIS BOOK FOCUSES on dunk tank survivors, we also would like to dedicate this book to all of those who are in education for the right reasons and who serve and are intentional about making a positive impact on our kids today. So many of our professional colleagues and personal friends are doing things the right way and are thriving in education.

We want to recognize the good cherries in the bunch and savor your commitment by encouraging you to keep doing what you are doing—you are the ones who may have helped us out of the tank whether you realize it or not. Every LinkedIn post, encouraging Twitter quote, dialogue in a blog, and informational YouTube video has contributed to the think tank that continues to impact our field, and, for that, we are grateful. We want to leave you with one final narrative from Simon Owens, a sixth-grade student in New Jersey, who drives our continued dunk tank work:

> *Mr. Randall is a super cool guy. He used to come into my classes and work with us on our science experiments, vocabulary Fridays, and so many other activities. Overall, I would say he is a good principal. He likes us. He respects us. He listens to us too. But something doesn't seem right with Mr. Randall lately. I see teachers whispering in the hallway. They are acting weird too. Not sure what it is about, but everyone seems off their rockers. It's like a ghost town around here [at school]. It's like someone died. A funeral. Yeah, that's what it's like: a funeral. I heard one of the teachers say something about Mr. Randall's tenure. I don't know what that even means, but Mr. Randall is not the same. That I know.*

Kids *notice* and *know* what is going on, and they push on the elephant's rear too! They *hear* things. They *see* things. They also know the mantra, *Do what's right and give it your best, because life is the most meaningful test.* They bought into it because you believed in it. They know some of the things that we think are only *adult* things. In this case, the reality of Mr. Randall not getting a recommendation from his superintendent for tenure to continue on as Simon's principal is real. And for Simon, the dunk tank effects are *noticeable.* Mr. Randall is facing a dunk tank blitzkrieg from his superintendent and two school board members because of an issue of bullying that took place on the playground a few months ago that Mr. Randall's adversaries feel was handled poorly.

We know it's hard to put forth the best *you* that you can offer even when things are maddening. But you have to. You have to try as hard as you can. You matter. You make a difference. Your students, teachers, community, and fellow leaders are watching, and they are learning from you.

You have an incredible opportunity to teach your students about what a dunk tank means. Teach them that life is complicated and that there are ways to navigate through any kind of dunk tank scenario without compromising your character or work ethic. They have their own adolescent dunk tanks going on and they need good examples for how to prevail. Your example and mentoring can help them grow into capable, coping, brilliantly skilled, and emotionally intelligent adults who just might become future educators or school leaders. Now go out there and be the best possible version of yourself. Be the change that you want to see.

—

We invite you to share your stories with us as featured on School Leaders Now (schoolleadersnow.com). Each week, we will feature a different leader's story and provide reflective thought, productive support, and sound advice. The site also offers access to resources and tools that we've collected and created just for you. Our reflection guide may be a support to you for leading a book study or facilitating a learning group. We want to continue the conversation and continue to feature *real* stories from *real* educators like you! Visit us at leadershipdunktank.com and share your story!

BRING THE DUNK TANK TO YOUR SCHOOL OR DISTRICT!

RICK AND REBECCA (**R&R**) are committed to helping your organization push on the elephant and learn more about relevant topics such as school leadership best practices, helping teachers, teens, and children avoid their own dunk tanks, or working with parents on how to better understand the field of education as it relates to politics, capacity building, and relationship building.

Rebecca and Rick offer tag-team keynote speaking engagements, workshops, and seminars that will help you, your administrative team, your teachers, and your students to fend off adversarial attacks and work together more effectively. To date, their audiences have laughed (not cried yet—thank goodness!), wondered, reflected, and been inspired to start a revolution for improving the educational landscape! Wait until you hear the stories that they share!

Topics that Rick and Rebecca address with schools include (but are not limited to):

- Leadership best practices
- Mindfulness in the classroom
- Technology innovation
- Best practices for hiring staff
- Curriculum development and learning standards
- School reform strategies and building a culture of kindness
- Teaching students about the metaphorical "dunk tank" that they will encounter in their lives . . . and much, much more!

LEARN MORE AT LEADERSHIPDUNKTANK.COM.

Don't wait to get *dunked*!
*Remember, there is always someone
who might want to throw balls
at your dunk tank target!
Invite R&R to work with your team today!*

MORE FROM

DAVE BURGESS
Consulting, Inc.

Teach Like a PIRATE

Increase Student Engagement, Boost Your Creativity, and Transform Your Life as an Educator

By Dave Burgess (@BurgessDave)

Teach Like a PIRATE is the *New York Times'* best-selling book that has sparked a worldwide educational revolution. It is part inspirational manifesto that ignites passion for the profession, and part practical road map filled with dynamic strategies to dramatically increase student engagement. Translated into multiple languages, its message resonates with educators who want to design outrageously creative lessons and transform school into a life-changing experience for students.

Learn Like a PIRATE

Empower Your Students to Collaborate, Lead, and Succeed

By Paul Solarz (@PaulSolarz)

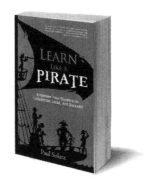

Today's job market demands that students be prepared to take responsibility for their lives and careers. We do them a disservice if we teach them how to earn passing grades without equipping them to take charge of their education. In *Learn Like a PIRATE*, Paul Solarz explains how to design classroom experiences that encourage students to take risks and explore their passions in a stimulating, motivating, and supportive environment where improvement, rather than grades, is the focus. Discover how student-led classrooms help students thrive and develop into self-directed, confident citizens who are capable of making smart, responsible decisions, all on their own.

P is for PIRATE

Inspirational ABC's for Educators

By Dave and Shelley Burgess (@Burgess_Shelley)

Teaching is an adventure that stretches the imagination and calls for creativity every day! In *P is for Pirate*, husband and wife team, Dave and Shelley Burgess, encourage and inspire educators to make their classrooms fun and exciting places to learn. Tapping into years of personal experience and drawing on the insights of more than seventy educators, the authors offer a wealth of ideas for making learning and teaching more fulfilling than ever before.

Play Like a Pirate

Engage Students with Toys, Games, and Comics

by Quinn Rollins (@jedikermit)

Yes! School can be simultaneously fun and educational. In *Play Like a Pirate*, Quinn Rollins offers practical, engaging strategies and resources that make it easy to integrate fun into your curriculum. Regardless of the grade level you teach, you'll find inspiration and ideas that will help you engage your students in unforgettable ways.

eXPlore Like a Pirate

Gamification and Game-Inspired Course Design to Engage, Enrich, and Elevate Your Learners

By Michael Matera (@MrMatera)

Are you ready to transform your classroom into an experiential world that flourishes on collaboration and creativity? Then set sail with classroom game designer and educator Michael Matera as he reveals the possibilities and power of game-based learning. In *eXPlore Like a Pirate*, Matera serves as your experienced guide to help you apply the most motivational techniques of gameplay to your classroom. You'll learn gamification strategies that will work with and enhance (rather than replace) your current curriculum and discover how these engaging methods can be applied to any grade level or subject.

Pure Genius

*Building a Culture of Innovation and
Taking 20% Time to the Next Level*

By Don Wettrick (@DonWettrick)

For far too long, schools have been bastions of boredom, killers of creativity, and way too comfortable with compliance and conformity. In *Pure Genius*, Don Wettrick explains how collaboration—with experts, students, and other educators—can help you create interesting, and even life-changing, opportunities for learning. Wettrick's book inspires and equips educators with a systematic blueprint for teaching innovation in any school.

The Zen Teacher

*Creating Focus, Simplicity, and
Tranquility in the Classroom*

By Dan Tricarico (@thezenteacher)

Teachers have incredible power to influence—even improve—the future. In *The Zen Teacher,* educator, blogger, and speaker Dan Tricarico provides practical, easy-to-use techniques to help teachers be their best—unrushed and fully focused—so they can maximize their performance and improve their quality of life. In this introductory guide, Dan Tricarico explains what it means to develop a Zen practice—something that has nothing to do with religion and everything to do with your ability to thrive in the classroom.

140 Twitter Tips for Educators

*Get Connected, Grow Your Professional Learning
Network, and Reinvigorate Your Career*

By Brad Currie, Billy Krakower, and Scott Rocco
(@bradmcurrie, @wkrakower, @ScottRRocco)

Whatever questions you have about education or about how you can be even better at your job, you'll find ideas, resources, and a vibrant network of professionals ready to help you on Twitter. In *140 Twitter Tips for Educators*, #Satchat hosts and founders of Evolving Educators, Brad Currie, Billy Krakower, and Scott Rocco offer step-by-step instructions to help you master the basics of Twitter, build an online following, and become a Twitter rock star.

The Innovator's Mindset

Empower Learning, Unleash Talent, and Lead a Culture of Creativity

By George Couros (@gcouros)

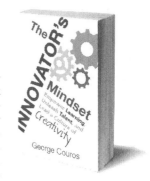

The traditional system of education requires students to hold their questions and compliantly stick to the scheduled curriculum. But our job as educators is to provide new and better opportunities for our students. It's time to recognize that compliance doesn't foster innovation, encourage critical thinking, or inspire creativity—and those are the skills our students need to succeed. In *The Innovator's Mindset*, George Couros encourages teachers and administrators to empower their learners to wonder, to explore—and to become forward-thinking leaders.

50 Things You Can Do with Google Classroom

By Alice Keeler and Libbi Miller
(@alicekeeler, @MillerLibbi)

It can be challenging to add new technology to the classroom but it's a must if students are going to be well-equipped for the future. Alice Keeler and Libbi Miller shorten the learning curve by providing a thorough overview of the Google Classroom App. Part of Google Apps for Education (GAfE), Google Classroom was specifically designed to help teachers save time by streamlining the process of going digital. Complete with screenshots, *50 Things You Can Do with Google Classroom* provides ideas and step-by-step instructions to help teachers implement this powerful tool.

50 Things to Go Further with Google Classroom

A Student-Centered Approach
By Alice Keeler and Libbi Miller
(@alicekeeler, @MillerLibbi)

Today's technology empowers educators to move away from the traditional classroom where teachers lead and students work independently— each doing the same thing. In 50 Things to Go Further with Google Classroom: A Student-Centered Approach, authors and educators Alice Keeler and Libbi Miller offer inspiration and resources to help you create a digitally rich, engaging, student-centered environment. They show you how to tap into the power of individualized learning that is possible with Google Classroom.

Master the Media

*How Teaching Media Literacy Can
Save Our Plugged-in World*

By Julie Smith (@julnilsmith)

Written to help teachers and parents educate the next generation, *Master the Media* explains the history, purpose, and messages behind the media. The point isn't to get kids to unplug; it's to help them make informed choices, understand the difference between truth and lies, and discern perception from reality. Critical thinking leads to smarter decisions—and it's why media literacy can save the world.

The Writing on the Classroom Wall

*How Posting Your Most Passionate Beliefs about
Education Can Empower Your Students, Propel Your
Growth, and Lead to a Lifetime of Learning*

By Steve Wyborney (@SteveWyborney)

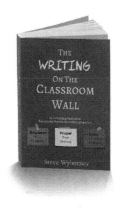

In *The Writing on the Classroom Wall*, Steve Wyborney explains how posting and discussing Big Ideas can lead to deeper learning. You'll learn why sharing your ideas will sharpen and refine them. You'll also be encouraged to know that the Big Ideas you share don't have to be profound to make a profound impact on learning. In fact, Steve explains, it's okay if some of your ideas fall *off* the wall. What matters most is sharing them.

Kids Deserve It!

*Pushing Boundaries and Challenging
Conventional Thinking*

By Todd Nesloney and Adam Welcome
(@TechNinjaTodd, @awelcome)

In *Kids Deserve It!*, Todd and Adam encourage you to think big and make learning fun and meaningful for students. Their high-tech, high-touch, and highly engaging practices will inspire you to take risks, shake up the status quo, and be a champion for your students. While you're at it, you just might rediscover why you became an educator in the first place.

The Classroom Chef

*Sharpen your lessons. Season your classes.
Make math meaningful.*

By John Stevens and Matt Vaudrey
(@Jstevens009, @MrVaudrey)

In *The Classroom Chef*, math teachers and instructional coaches John Stevens and Matt Vaudrey share their secret recipes, ingredients, and tips for serving up lessons that engage students and help them "get" math. You can use these ideas and methods as-is, or better yet, tweak them and create your own enticing educational meals. The message the authors share is that, with imagination and preparation, every teacher can be a Classroom Chef.

Ditch That Textbook

*Free Your Teaching and Revolutionize
Your Classroom*

By Matt Miller (@jmattmiller)

Textbooks are symbols of centuries-old education. They're often outdated as soon as they hit students' desks. Acting "by the textbook" implies compliance and a lack of creativity. It's time to ditch those textbooks—and those textbook assumptions about learning! In *Ditch That Textbook*, teacher and blogger Matt Miller encourages educators to throw out meaningless, pedestrian teaching and learning practices. He empowers them to evolve and improve on old, standard, teaching methods. *Ditch That Textbook* is a support system, toolbox, and manifesto to help educators free their teaching and revolutionize their classrooms.

Your School Rocks ... So Tell People!

*Passionately Pitch and Promote the Positives
Happening on Your Campus*

By Ryan McLane and Eric Lowe
(@McLane_Ryan, @EricLowe21)

Great things are happening in your school every day. The problem is, no one beyond your school walls knows about them. School principals Ryan McLane and Eric Lowe want to help you get the word out! In *Your School Rocks ... So Tell People!* McLane and Lowe offer more than seventy immediately actionable tips along with easy-to-follow instructions and links to video tutorials. This practical guide will equip you to create an effective and manageable communication strategy using social media tools. Learn how to keep your students' families and community connected, informed, and excited about what's going on in your school.

How Much Water Do We Have?

*5 Success Principles for Conquering Any
Change and Thriving in Times of Change*

By Pete Nunweiler with Kris Nunweiler

In *How Much Water Do We Have?* Pete Nunweiler identifies five key elements—information, planning, motivation, support, and leadership—that are necessary for the success of any goal, life transition, or challenge. Referring to these elements as the 5 Waters of Success, Pete explains that like the water we drink, you need them to thrive in today's rapidly paced world. If you're feeling stressed out, overwhelmed, or uncertain at work or at home, pause and look for the signs of dehydration. Learn how to find, acquire, and use the 5 Waters of Success—so you can share them with your team and family members.

Launch

*Using Design Thinking to Boost Creativity
and Bring Out the Maker in Every Student*

By John Spencer and A.J. Juliani (@spencerideas, @ajjuliani)

Something happens in students when they define themselves as *makers* and *inventors* and *creators*. They discover powerful skills—problem-solving, critical thinking, and imagination—that will help them shape the world's future … *our* future. In *LAUNCH*, John Spencer and A.J. Juliani provide a process that can be incorporated into every class at every grade level … even if you don't consider yourself a "creative teacher." And if you dare to innovate and view creativity as an essential skill, you will empower your students to change the world—starting right now.

Instant Relevance

Using Today's Experiences in Tomorrow's Lessons

By Denis Sheeran (@MathDenisNJ)

Every day, students in schools around the world ask the question, "When am I ever going to use this in real life?" In *Instant Relevance*, author and keynote speaker Denis Sheeran equips you to create engaging lessons from experiences and events that matter to your students. Learn how to help your students see meaningful connections between the real word and what they learn in the classroom—because that's when learning sticks.

A BIT ABOUT
REBECCA
AND RICK

R EBECCA CODA, M.A. ED, is a National Board Certified Teacher, recognized Master Teacher through the
Arizona K–12 Center, ELA curriculum and assessment
writer, and technology program leader in Phoenix, Arizona.
She is the founder of the Digital Native Network as the website
author, blogger, and curriculum resources designer.

Rebecca has experienced the school leader's dunk tank first hand. As an outlet for prevailing in her suffocating situation, she decided to augment her passion and love for teaching by creating and sharing resources available on her website, writing inspirational articles, connecting on LinkedIn and Twitter, and working on more manuscripts. In addition to co-authoring additional upcoming books in the *Dunk Tank* Series, she is working on her latest work, *Life Trapped,* which will focus on prevailing spiritually. Rebecca serves her community as a STEM Coach and a special needs volunteer for children at her local church. She has wanted to be a teacher all her life, incessantly role played being a teacher (lining up her dolls in "class" since her first day of kindergarten), and has worked in the field of education for eighteen years. Rebecca is happily married to her husband Mike, with whom she shares three talented, beautiful, entertaining, and brilliant children they have adopted from the foster system. Together they share six (yes, SIX) dogs—a Rhodesian Ridgeback (Sadie) and five wiener dogs (Jock, Maggie, Baron, Zeke, and Halo). Life is never boring!

For more information about Rebecca's other projects, speaking engagement topics, or resources please visit: rebeccacoda.com or digitalnativenetwork.net. You may contact Rebecca Coda directly at info@digitalnativenetwork.net and on LinkedIn and Twitter @RebeccaCoda #SLDUNKTANK.

RICK JETTER, PH.D., is an educational consultant for K–12 schools across the nation. He is the author of *Hiring the Best Staff for Your School, The Isolate /n./, Sutures of the Mind,* and *Igniting Wonder, Reflection, and Change in Our Schools.* Rick is also currently writing seven new manuscripts, four of which will be authored with Rebecca Coda for their dunk tank series for kids and teachers, and a fifth that has to do with the "Internet of things" in education.

Rick serves the educational community as the Director of K–12 Education for Advanced Educational Products (AEP), which is a leading educational resources company in the nation (Note: If you work in a school district or university and don't know about AEP, you have to check them out at: aepk12.com).

Rick coaches writers and authors across various industries, including education, the health/sciences field, and the business sector. He has previously worked in the field of education for more than eighteen years. He started his career as an alternative education teacher before becoming a middle school English teacher. He has held public school leadership positions, including middle school assistant principal, elementary school principal, assistant superintendent of human resources, assistant superintendent of technology, and superintendent of schools. Rick has an incredible wife named Jennifer and three cool kids named Eddie, Nora, and Ellen. Timothy is Rick's stepson, with his two grandkids, Dale and Emmett, and Suzi, his daughter-in-law. Rick's family dog is named George. Yes, that's right: George Jetter, not George Jetson.

Rick has experienced the school leader's dunk tank first-hand before pursuing a career of educational consulting, speaking, writing, and publishing.

For more information about Rick's other projects and speaking engagement topics, please plug-in to Dr. J. by visiting rickjetter.com. You may also contact Rick directly at drjetter1@gmail.com and on LinkedIn and Twitter @RickJetter #SLDUNKTANK. More about this book and future dunk tank projects can be found at leadershipdunktank.com. You can also download our free Reflection Guide that accompanies this book.

44759689R00155

Made in the USA
Middletown, DE
15 June 2017